The Little Professional P.I.N.K. Book of Success

Erica Moore-Burton, Esq.

MONDAY SMILES

Los Angeles

The Little Professional P.I.N.K. Book of Success

Copyright © 2010 by Erica Moore-Burton

No part of this book may be used or reproduced in any manner whatsoever without the written permission from the publisher except in the case of brief excerpts embodied in critical articles and reviews.

Published by: Monday Smiles, LLC
                     www.mondaysmiles.com
                     P.O. Box 480293
                     Los Angeles, CA 90048

Library of Congress Cataloging-in-Publication Data

Moore-Burton, Erica, 1974-
The Little Professional P.I.N.K. Book of Success

ISBN 978-0-615-31303-0
LCCN 2009907817

Typesetting and text design: Rising Ambitions Media Group
(www.risingambitions.com)
Editors: Rising Ambitions Media Group and Copypolish

Cover design by Raymond Floyd (www.jussray.com)

Printed and Manufactured in the United States

Contents

Acknowledgments

Thank you to my loving husband, Chappale Linn Burton, whose encouragement, spirit, and example help me to be a better person every single day I walk on this amazing earth.

Also, thank you to my parents, Trevor and Margaret Moore. I wouldn't be where I am without your love and support. You both sacrificed and worked hard over the years to build a strong foundation for each of your girls. You gave me the confidence to dream and the education (both traditional and emotional) to do whatever I put my mind to. I am grateful to you both every day, and I love you.

Dedication

...who had a strong influence on my life by demonstrating the P.I.N.K. principles throughout hers...

Introduction

The goal of the Little Professional P.I.N.K. Book series is to provide you with a short but informative read that will help you in your personal and professional journey. These books are intended for women who want more out of their lives and careers. I know that time is limited—you've got places to go, people to see and things to do—so these little books are intended to be read and re-read in short sessions. You can read perhaps while you're getting a pedicure, having your hair done, riding the train to work, or enjoying your lunch break!

I came across an interesting fact while writing this book. Did you know that one third of people never pick up another book after graduating from high school, and 42 percent of college graduates never read another book after college? These statistics are mind-boggling. Taking that into account, I wanted to write something that would be of value to the avid reader as well as pique the interest of others who don't read as much. My goal is to make these little books as succinct as possible while providing lots of information that will help you reach your next level of success. At the end of this book I have provided a list of further resources that I have found helpful over the years. Enjoy!

chapter 1

Success

Those of you who have attended my seminars or workshops already know the principles I live by. They are what I call the P.I.N.K. principles, and they are explained and explored throughout the Little Professional P.I.N.K. Book series. You can carry these principles through your career—whether you are just stepping onto the corporate ladder in an entry-level position, whether you are midway through your career, or whether you are reaching the end of your career. For those who may not be familiar with these principles, I'll briefly explain.

Over the years, the color pink has become more than just a pretty color. Pink is the color that symbolizes awareness of women fighting breast cancer. There is also a best-selling artist named Pink, whose spunk and music make you want to conquer the world! Pink is also the name of a sensual Victoria Secret brand that makes women feel sexy all day long! The list goes on.

P.I.N.K. has come to be symbolic for women making things happen in their careers and in the workplace. With P.I.N.K., you can do anything, be anybody, and go anywhere. The P stands for PASSION, I for INTEGRITY, N for No Limits, and K for KNOWLEDGE. You will find these principles woven throughout this book and the series, and I hope to explore them more when I meet you at one of my workshops!

What is Success?

What is success? That's a really interesting question isn't it? Is success Beyonce? Is success Mother Teresa, Oprah Winfrey, or Hillary Clinton? I'm sure that you would consider all of these women successful. However, consider these individuals: an independent woman who raises a son with Down syndrome; a woman who paints pictures that are displayed in a local gallery; a woman who finishes a marathon; or a woman who helps her company operate more efficiently and achieve growth year over year. You may or may not consider these women's lives to be success stories; it really depends on your definition of success. For many, success is being famous and in the public eye, for some it is making a lot of money, and for others it is being a good mother. The point is that success comes in many different shapes and sizes. Success is a goal that many try to achieve without really putting a definition on it for themselves. Success is certainly subjective. What I define as success may not match someone else's definition of success.

My definition of success is:
Setting personal goals that are in line with my passion and purpose, and moving toward the desired outcome.

Again, this is my definition of success. Your definition may be different, and that is the key here: you have to define what success is for you. Success for you could be accumulating a certain amount of wealth, planting a garden that blooms in the spring, or creating an invention that changes the world.

Although all of us may have different definitions of success, I think we can agree that striving toward our goals is a success in itself. Each step is an important milestone. What I mean by that is, for me to be successful in losing weight, I need to stick to my diet and exercise three times a week. For me to be successful in writing a book, I need to finish four chapters a week. Also, as an author, if I am able to help one person on her journey to reach a goal, then I have been successful in delivering my message.

2

> "Once I decide to do something, I can't have
> people telling me I can't. If there's a roadblock,
> you jump over it, walk around it, crawl under it."
>
> — **Kitty Kelley**

I'm sure you've heard the phrase: "The rich get richer and the poor get poorer." Well, I have discovered that the same philosophy applies to success. Have you ever noticed that successful people seem to continue to be successful? One good thing after another just happens to them: they get one promotion after another, or one great opportunity after another. This is why it is imperative to set small, manageable, realistic, and achievable goals. As you begin to be successful in achieving smaller goals, you will also become more and more successful meeting larger ones. You will begin to find that life will offer you more in terms of success and start presenting you with new opportunities every step of the way. Always remember that phrase. It is one of my favorite mantras.

Success Attracts Success

Do you want to be the next Suzie Orman? I am a believer in dreaming big, so I think that would be a great and admirable goal. You should start off by setting some smaller goals that all relate to your larger goal. For example, a short-term achievable and realistic goal may be to subscribe to the Wall Street Journal so that you can start to learn the language of finance. An even smaller goal may be to get your household finances in impeccable order. A long-term goal may be to research training programs at financial institutions. Keep setting short-term goals, and then step by step scale up to bigger ones. Again, as you achieve success in accomplishing smaller

3

tasks and short-term goals, bigger and greater success will inevitably follow. In the next section on goal setting, we are going to further examine how to accomplish your short-term goals while moving toward some of your long-term goals.

As you experience success with your smaller goals, make sure to take the time to stop, smell the roses, and celebrate! This is a very important ingredient in the success formula. You have to celebrate your successes, even if only in small ways. Today, I celebrated the fact that I did a four-mile run by enjoying a piece of berry pie from one of my favorite bakeries. I have used television shows, movies, walks, and CDs as small motivators to help me complete goals. So why is celebrating so important? Celebrating will encourage you to win more often. Remember the phrase: "Success attracts success."

Failure

I would be remiss if I didn't address failure. Failure is inevitable in life. On our journey to success, we will fail at some of the things we attempt. Failure is not a dirty word; in fact, I always use failure as a form of feedback and correction. Failure lets me know what not to do. The key to overcoming failure is in our response to it. Do we wallow in self-pity, or do we get back up and try again, with the knowledge of what not to do? Did you know that it took Thomas Edison 10,000 attempts before he was successful in creating the light bulb?? After he had made about 9,000 attempts, Edison was interviewed by a reporter who asked him if he felt he was a failure and should give up. Edison replied, "Young man, why would I feel like a failure? And why would I ever give up? I now know definitively over 9,000 ways that an electric light bulb will not work. Success is almost in my grasp." After 1,000 more attempts, he created the light bulb! I have failed at many things, but I have used my failures as a guide through the maze of life. Envision a life-sized maze. Every failure for me has been a wall, and when I have hit that wall in the past I have simply turned around to look for an opening. Often it has been very close by. Failure can be a great character builder, depending on how you respond to it. It can build the muscle of perseverance within you; and when you have perseverance, you can do anything and become anyone you want.

> "Perseverance is failing nineteen times and succeeding on the twentith." - Julie Andrews

Success Starts With a Great Attitude

Success starts with a great attitude. I have a plaque in my home office that states the following:

"Attitude Is Everything"

EXERCISE

I read my plaque almost every day and remember that, above anything else, the one thing that I get to choose every day is my attitude. Here's a good quick exercise. **Write a list of the top five people in your life who you deem to be successful in some way.**

1. _____

2. _____

3. _____

4. _____

5. _____

What is it that makes these people successful? As you go through this book, look at the principles that I discuss and see which ones you recognize in these people. Especially take note of the individuals who have qualities that you would like to emulate.

Next, examine what their attitudes are like on a daily basis. How does this relate to the successful parts of their lives? I don't know the five people you have listed above, but I would guess these individuals take full responsibility and ownership over the successful areas of their lives. Without even knowing them, I can guarantee these people have great attitudes and are probably passionate about the things that make them successful. The lesson here is that your attitude in life will most certainly determine your altitude in life.

So what does it mean to have a good attitude? It means that your outlook on life is that of seeing a glass as being half-full, not half-empty. Having a good attitude is about 'showing up' in life and being the best person you can be. It's about influencing the world around you in the best possible way you can. It's about taking responsibility for everything in your life from your career and finances to your relationships and health. Taking responsibility is a huge component of success, but it is often overlooked. (I will discuss this concept more in another chapter of this book.) Over the years in my personal and professional life, I have come across many individuals who refuse to take responsibility in their lives; then, they wonder why unfortunate things always seem to happen to them, or why they just can't seem to get ahead in the area of their life where they are struggling. Taking responsibility is one of the first steps to success. You are the only person who can take responsibility for your actions and determine whether or not your life is going to be successful. Let's put it in simple terms. Things that are beyond your control are going to happen during your journey. Some of these

6

things will be both unfortunate and unfair, but there is one thing you will have control over, and that is your response (your attitude). It's so easy to blame others for your lack of career opportunities, lack of finances, poor health and relationships, or anything else that you see as preventing success in your life. Taking responsibility is one of the golden keys to attaining higher levels of success in any area of your life.

> "We are taught you must blame your fathers, your sisters, your brothers, the school, the teachers – you can blame anyone, but never blame yourself. It's never your fault. But it's always your fault, because if you want to change, you're the one who has got to change. It's as simple as that, isn't it?"
>
> **- Katherine Hepburn**

You are in control of the one thing that is needed to be successful, and that is your attitude. That is the one thing you get to choose and control on a daily basis. If you often find yourself blaming your boss, co-workers, company, friends, spouse, parents, or siblings for things that are not right in your life, you are probably someone who is not taking responsibility. From this day forward, I challenge you to stop blaming and start taking responsibility - NOW! Whatever challenges come your way, whatever obstacles arise, if you find a way to take responsibility, you will also find a way to take control of your life.

> "In the long run, we shape our lives and we shape ourselves. The process never ends until we die. And the choices we make are ultimately our own responsibility."   **- Eleanor Roosevelt**

Passion

We mentioned earlier that passion is an attribute of success. Passion is a key ingredient. It is the thing that drives you all the way to the front door of success. Passion is that feeling of absolute desire to be, perform, and execute. It is that "thing" that excites you about your goal and that feeling of nirvana when you're in the middle of being, doing, and performing. Passion gets you up in the morning, ready to take on the day with zest and excitement. If you ever look at children between the ages of about two and eight, you will find they wake up in the morning ready to go and play in the game of life. They can't wait to be around all the toys, the colors, their parents, the outdoors, their friends, and sticky sweet foods! Most of them are passionate little beings. Unfortunately, many of us don't live passionate lives, because we fall victim to circumstance. A job falls in our lap, and we take it because it pays the bills, provides good benefits, or for some other reason. We often forget the most important reason for taking a job, which is that we feel passionate about doing it. We then clock in and clock out on a daily basis, having lost sight of all that is important and that which leads to greater heights of success. Many people are locked into a false belief that they can't live a life of passion and that passion is just for celebrities or the super wealthy. This kind of thought process is detrimental to your success and your life.

"Never underestimate the power of passion."

- **Eve Sawyer**

I am sure many of you have heard the adage: "When you do what you're passionate about, you'll never have to work a day in your life." What does that really mean? "You'll never have to work a day in your life." I'm sure there are people in your life who live truly passionate lives. They are excited to wake up in the morning and are essentially like the children I described earlier. We see it in some famous people, like Venus and Serena Williams, Oprah Winfrey, Beyonce, Suzie Orman, and Barbara Walters. When I studied the lives of these women, I discovered they live with passion and purpose; they're in their element and are very successful as a by-product.

I recall a time when I was working in a law firm many years ago. I had been there for a few years and worked in a small, dim office without any windows. My day-to-day duties consisted of drafting incorporation documents for companies, filing them with the court, and drafting more documents for the purchase and sale of commercial real estate. Yawn, yawn, and yawn! Don't get me wrong, there is nothing wrong with this type of work. For some it is very fulfilling. But, anyone that knows me knows that I'm not cut out for small offices and detailed paperwork. I'm more of the social butterfly type that needs to be out and about interacting with people. I had been with the firm for three years, and going to work had become painful for me. It was painful getting up; it was painful being there; it was painful putting an act on for the attorneys; and, it was an absolute JOY to go home. I would leave at exactly five o' clock (not a minute later). I clearly wasn't living my passion. In time, it started to affect my health, happiness, and general well-being. I was just doing the work that I was being paid to do, but I wasn't doing it with passion. I certainly wasn't being fair to my employers. Even more important, I wasn't being fair to myself. Finally, I reached my pain threshold. One day, I made the statement to a friend, "I would rather be lying in a hospital bed than go to the office." I knew at that point that it was time to leave...

ready or not. At the end of the day, whatever we focus on expands, and we become what we think about most of the time. If I had continued in that frame of mind, I hate to think what could have happened to me. Do you think I was successful in this role? I was doing the work that was assigned to me and making great money, but could I truly be deemed "successful"? Well, the answer is obviously no. How can true success be a by-product if you're not doing the work with integrity and passion?

Success is not just about money. I was making great money at the time. I had received a considerable jump in salary when I moved from a previous position, and I was driving a beautiful, new, sleek, black sports car. I lived in a great apartment in a desirable part of town, and I was using my vacation time to travel all over the world. However, I wasn't passionate about what I was doing for 8 hours of the day. I was pretty much going through the motions, and what I was doing most of the time, wasn't in line with my heart's desire. To any onlooker, I had all the accoutrements of success, but in my heart, I wasn't happy. Therefore, I certainly wasn't successful.

When I left the firm, I decided to take a break, a sabbatical of sorts. I decided not to work for six months to figure out what I needed to do. During this time, I did some in-depth introspection to uncover what my core values were and what job or career would be in line with some of my natural talents. In other words, I sought to discover what I would enjoy being paid for AND, most important, what I would be passionate about.

The process took about two months. During those two months, I read a number of books (some of which are listed in the back of this book). Every day, I spent time answering questions about my life, my dreams and aspirations as a young child, observations that had been made about me at all my previous jobs, at school, and university. It

10

was such a refreshing, effective and enlightening process that I now use it as the foundation for one of the P.I.N.K. coaching programs. It's funny how I even reflected on my school days and remembered when my math teacher, Mr. Clarke, threw a piece of chalk at me to get my attention and tell me to stop talking. I even thought about the time when I worked at a shoe shop at the age of 16 and was fired after a few months for "talking too much." I had been so upset at the time, but looking back at the experience more than 15 years later, I discovered that my tendency to talk too much was actually a strength I should be using! I obviously needed to be in a position where I could talk to people; because obviously that was something I enjoyed doing. Through further examination, I found out that it was something that I needed to do and would benefit from doing as a large component of my career.

If you are having a challenging time trying to find what your passion is, here are a few simple exercises you can do right now.

PASSION EXERCISES

1. List all of the jobs that you have had over the course of your life.
2. Put an asterisk next to each job that you really enjoyed.
3. List all of your current hobbies.
4. Place an asterisk next to your top two hobbies.
5. List your top five skills (e.g. writing, oral communication, management, etc.)
6. Go back to the jobs that have an asterisk next to them and write down exactly what you enjoyed about those jobs. Was there a high level of interaction with people? Did you enjoy preparing detailed paperwork, planning events, devising complex strategies, engaging in creative writing, or performing customer service? Write everything down.
7. Look at all of the positions that you didn't like, and make a list of what exactly you disliked about them.
8. Now, line up what you liked about the positions with your hobbies and look for common themes. Can you marry any of the things that you have enjoyed about certain jobs with your hobbies (if they are hobbies that you would enjoy getting paid for)?

11

These exercises are not meant to be completed in 10 or 20 minutes. Carve out a minimum of two to four hours (or even dedicate a whole weekend) to really dig deep to discover some of your passion points. These are the keys to your success. Imagine if you could find your passion and change paths in months instead of years, as many people tend to do. For me, I figured out that I had to be around people; that was a must. I also discovered that I enjoyed helping people and seeing the direct results of my contributions. Also, I finally came to the realization that interaction and communication, a.k.a. "talking" was a large component for me. What many people throughout my life may have deemed to be negative could actually be turned into something positive.

At the time I was doing this self-assessment, I also realized that I had always been a phone person. If I wasn't sleeping or working, you would typically find me engaged in a conversation on the telephone. Well, after continuing to study and assess my strengths, weaknesses, values, desires, and hobbies, I found that executive recruiting (using my legal background) could be a good option for me. After doing some research about the profession, I embarked upon that career path, and it was no surprise that I was successful almost immediately. I was using all of my natural talents, working in line with my core values, and I felt passionate about what I was doing on a day–to-day basis. I went on to help thousands of people (and to this day I still hear about the positive effects that I had on their lives). In just a few years I became the recipient of many awards for my sales and leadership achievements, joined the One Million Dollar Club, and I went on to make more money than I'd ever made in my life before. At 28 years old, I was happy in my heart, living a successful life, and had stepped up into a very healthy six-figure income.

"Happiness must be cultivated. It is like character. It is not a thing to be safely let alone for a moment, or it will run to weeds."

- Elizabeth Stuart Phelps

Part of being successful is taking the time to conduct a self-assessment. I have just taken you through a very simple one here. There are many self-assessment books on the market, and you can find a lot of free self-assessment material online. What is imperative for your success is to take time out to continually engage in self-assessments. Any time you feel your interest waning, or you feel that you are no longer passionate about what you're doing, take the time to do an assessment. Every few years, I conduct a self-assessment. If you are not the disciplined type, it would be a worthwhile investment to hire a career or life coach to help you. It's interesting how we are quick to join an exercise class or get a fitness coach for our physical bodies, or to get the help of a therapist when we're having emotional problems, but hesitate to employ a coach for our careers and lives in general. A career/life coach can certainly help you get to the next level more quickly than you ever imagined, and can be the best investment of time and money for a more fulfilling and rewarding life.

"Freedom is knowing who you really are."

- Linda Thomson

To be successful and realize your full potential, you have to be willing and brave enough to play all out. Playing all out means that you are living life to the fullest, taking risks, taking advantage of opportunities, trying new things, meeting new people, and traveling to new places.

13

The concept that I love to use in my seminars is that of the "expiration date." Food has an expiration date, the day that the food is required to be taken off the shelf and disposed of. What is your expiration date? Many of us don't know when our expiration date is, but one thing holds true, and that is we all have one. It could be tomorrow; it could be next week or next year. We all have an expiration date that is etched into our hearts with invisible ink. One day it will stop beating, and it will be our turn to be taken off the shelf of life. The one regret that many older people have about their lives is that they didn't live it to their fullest potential; they didn't take enough risks and didn't go for it when they had the opportunity to do so. Don't let that be you. Let your light shine and go for your dreams, one step at a time.

> "You've got to sing like you don't need the money. You've got to love like you'll never get hurt. You've got to dance like nobody's watching. You've got to come from the heart, if you want it to work."
> — Susanna Clark

I'm not suggesting that you take a haphazard approach, but you must take the first step, even if that may be uncomfortable for you. For example, if you paint as a hobby, and you've never had a show before, it may feel uncomfortable to go to a few small, local galleries and ask them about exhibiting some pieces of your work. However, the worse thing they can say is "no." And, even if that happens to be the case, you haven't really lost anything. If they do say no, engage them in a conversation about the local art scene and see if you can garner some information that will help you on your path. Perhaps you can rent an empty space for an evening and put on your own show or even turn your home into a gallery for the evening and invite your friends and their friends! Even if you have your first show at a friend's home, everyone has to start somewhere. As Goethe said, "There is magic in boldness."

Most people are very successful in one area of their lives and not in others. Sit and ask yourself questions about where you are now and where you would like to be. If you don't feel that you can get yourself there alone, ask others for help. None of us are islands; we all need help in one form or another during our lives. Yet, at times we think that asking for help to take the next step up the ladder is indicative of weakness. Did you know that Hillary Clinton has a speech coach, and the world famous professional golfer Lorena Ochoa has several coaches? Even people who are the best in their fields have coaches. So, if you feel that asking for help is a weakness, change your mindset immediately!

> "She who is afraid of asking is afraid of learning."
> — Danish proverb

Mindset

My friend Tracy has a story that is similar to mine. Tracy worked at one of the big four auditing companies in the middle of downtown Manhattan. To many onlookers, she had a successful career. She made great money, did a great job at work day to day, and had a wonderful lifestyle. Inside, however, she was miserable. She did her job well, because she had to make a living. Her parents had always wanted her to be an accountant. Her heart's desire, however, was to open a bakery and spend her days cooking delectable cakes, scones, and other treats for people. She had fallen into corporate America, because that's what she thought she was supposed to do. She had succumbed to family and societal pressures to become a good corporate executive when she left college. For a while, she was pretty happy with her lot. However, over time Tracy reached her pain threshold, and it began to affect her health. When Tracy decided that it was time to make some changes, she didn't jump ship immediately, but she started to prepare herself for a change. The first thing she did was set some goals and timelines. Then, she started to prepare her mind for the transition she was going to make. Notice I said "going to make," not going to "try" to make. Tracy used a series of self-assessment exercises as her guide to transition and started to ready her mind, because she wanted to make that transition within six months.

The most important thing for her to prepare her mind had to do with reprogramming her thought patterns so that she could make the transition. We must remember that "success" is a mindset. When you have a "success" mindset, and it is applied to many areas of your life, amazing things can happen. To prepare your mind is to quiet the mind so that you can lay the groundwork for a paradigm shift. This is a strange concept for many people, because their minds are never quiet. From the moment they wake up in the morning to the moment they sleep at night, there is some kind of stimulation. Whether it's music or the television blaring, text messages on the BlackBerry, e-mails, thinking about the day ahead, thinking about yesterday, or worrying about the future, the mental noise is constant. Tracy's mind was one of those that was constantly on the go. The only downtime she had was when she was sleeping! The other issue Tracy faced was a lot of negative self-talk about why she couldn't make the transition. Internal messages, such as she wasn't good enough, she didn't know the first thing about running a bakery, or she wouldn't be able to make enough money to sustain herself would constantly run in a loop in her mind.

First things first, Tracy needed some quiet time every day to drastically adjust her mindset. She started by working with a coach who helped her incorporate daily meditation into her schedule. Just 10 to 20 minutes a day of complete silence, quietness, and stillness. At first she resisted, because it felt strange to her. But as she started to learn how to quiet her mind for two minutes, then three, then four, she began to reap the benefits. Her focus and discipline became a lot stronger, clearer, and easier to tap into. She also found that the stress and anxiety levels that she had associated with the move started to diminish. The second thing she did was start working on the negative self-talk. Tracy implemented the use of affirmations. When she heard her thoughts say phrases, like "I can't do this because I am not qualified," she started refocusing and purposely using positive phrases, like "I can do this because I have everything I need," "I am an intelligent person that can accomplish anything that I put my mind to," and "I am a successful business owner."

Meditation and affirmations can be key components to reaching peak success levels. Ask anyone who is at the peak of success if they use some form of meditation or affirmations. Whether they are aware of it or not, over 90% percent of highly successful individuals are using these kinds of mental tools.

Meditation can be found in many different forms. It doesn't necessarily mean sitting crossed-legged with your eyes closed, and hands positioned on your lap. Meditation can be in the form of doing yoga, chanting mantras, or simply focused breathing. Even quiet contemplation can be effective, and it can include gardening, walking, knitting, or a number of other activities. It is the quiet contemplation that is most important. Once the mind is quiet, you can start to think a lot more clearly about your life's direction. The continuous discipline can provide you with a key to success. Here are some of the affirmations I recite every day:

I am in excellent health.
Lucrative opportunities are continually attracted to me.
I am abundant.
I am a unique and successful being.
I have excellent focus and follow-through.
I create my life and my financial success.

I recite these affirmations among others every day. By doing this for the last seven years or so, I have made them a part of my belief system. Whenever anything happens to me during the day that is contrary to any of these affirmations, a positive phrase immediately enters my mind to refute it. For example, if I'm talking with someone who is lamenting about his or her financial affairs, saying, "Gosh, I'm so broke," the immediate affirmation that comes up in my mind is "Lucrative opportunities are continually attracted to me." I have refuted the negative statement. It literally hits a visual brick wall and it is replaced with one that is in line with my belief system. It certainly takes a lot of practice, because your natural inclination may be to agree with that person to make him or her feel more comfortable or join in by talking about your financial affairs in the same way. The key is to keep your mindset in the right place, and affirmations can be a very effective tool to do this. Bear in mind that meditation and affirmations aren't tools you use once and discard; they are most effective when they become a natural part of your lifestyle, and that takes practice.

> "I am optimistic and confident in all that I do. I affirm only the best for myself and others. I am the creator of my life and my world. I meet daily challenges gracefully and with complete confidence. I fill my mind with positive, nurturing, and healing thoughts."
>
> **- Alice Potter**

For Tracy, making a significant change in her mindset was a hard thing to grapple with. The use of meditation and affirmations was unlike anything she had ever done before.

But, as soon as she started using these amazing tools and committed to doing this for 21 days, she created a habit and started to see the benefits of the paradigm shift. She had finally started to replace her old belief system with a new one and started believing that she could in fact have anything she wanted, including her bakery.

> "A journey of a thousand miles must begin with a single step."
>
> **- Chinese proverb**

Part of being successful is knowing how to set goals and timelines. Tracy set herself up with a realistic six-month timeline and started to do something every day that would move her toward the end result. She would bake every week and use her co-workers' taste buds for valuable feedback. As a result, she began to refine her cooking techniques. By doing this, she used her current situation to help with her future aspirations. Often there are opportunities right where you are that help you learn or implement something that can help with your future. Sometimes you have to start right where you are, instead of jumping head first into your new endeavor (If you're

19

not familiar with the Acres of Diamonds story by Russell Conwell, go online and read it.) Tracy also enlisted the help of a mentor, someone that owned a bakery in another state. She started reading books recommended by that individual, and soon she had set goals for the creation of a business plan. Finally, the wheels were in motion for her new life. Six months later, she was decorating her new shop and had everything in place for a launch the following month. When we asked her what the keys were to making such a huge life change, she responded that the first step was to make a commitment to the end result. The second step was to believe that she could do it. The third was easy: it was to begin taking small steps toward the completion of her goal!

"The secret of getting ahead is getting started."

- Sally Berger

Throughout this book, we touch on some of the important concepts and ideas for success. This first chapter will get you started in laying a basic foundation for your own success. Here is a quick summary:

1. Create your own definition of success.
2. Wake up your passion to be successful!
3. Undertake a full and complete self-inventory of the things that you have done in your life to date, including jobs, hobbies, relationships, and other life events. Take an inventory of your general skills. Then dissect all the information and learn from it.
4. Take time out for contemplation, whether you use traditional meditation or some other technique.
5. Ensure your mindset is tuned to the right channel by using affirmations. The attainment of any level of success starts with the mind.
6. Make sure that you're playing the game of life and not standing on the sidelines.

20

chapter 2

Goal Setting

Goal setting is imperative to achieve any level of success in life. If you don't set goals, chances are you're not going to get very far. Further, it's not just a matter of setting goals; it's about working diligently toward their ultimate achievement. The reason many people do not stick to their goals is because they set unachievable goals or unrealistic timelines. When they do this, they fail to attain success, because they end up giving up too soon. If you're not setting solid goals for yourself, you have to ask yourself whether you are really reaching your full potential and living life to the fullest.

> "I look at victory as milestones on a very long highway."
> — Joan Benoit Samuelson

Those of you who have attended my seminars have heard me use the phrase "Step it up!" frequently. Well, this is the phrase that encapsulates this chapter on goal setting. Getting where you want to go in life may not be easy, and you may not have all the tools you need right now. However, what you do have is your attitude, and if your attitude is in the right place, all you need to do is "Step it up!" "Step it up" essentially means rise to the challenge; set your goals (both long- and short-term); plan carefully to create timelines; find your motivation and your passion; and then start taking one step at a time to work diligently toward your goals! There is only one person between you and the achievement of your goals, and that person is you. We can all make excuses as to why we can't do something; that is simply the easy way out. At times, we just don't know where to start. If that sounds like you, then enlist the help of others.

21

> "One only gets to the top rung of the ladder by steadily climbing up one at a time, and suddenly all sorts of powers, all sorts of abilities which you thought never belonged to you, suddenly become within your own possibility."
>
> **- Margaret Thatcher**

Try some of the techniques detailed in this book to help you set goals and get started. I've used many of them for years, and they have helped me reach levels of success I once only dreamed about. Once you set goals, have the resounding faith that the result is going to occur; stick to the plan; and STEP IT UP! If you do this, success is inevitable.

> "Be of good cheer. Do not think of today's failures but of the success that may come tomorrow. You have set yourselves a difficult task, but you will succeed if you persevere, and you will find a joy in overcoming obstacles. Remember, no effort that we make to attain something beautiful is ever lost."
>
> **- Helen Keller**

Whatever your goal is, you can start today by creating a plan. Whether you're an executive who wants to be a journalist or you're working as a dental assistant but really want to be the dentist, set the intention today. Grab a pencil and piece of paper and start to create a plan for your future. In the next section, I will outline some goal-setting techniques that have worked very well for me over the years. My hope is that you will start to use some of these techniques or different ones that work for you.

Step It Up! Using the Stepladder

Back in 2007, I ran a marathon. Less than 1 percent of the world's population will ever complete a marathon (26.2 miles). Actually, I never actually thought I would take on such an endeavor. I am certainly not a runner, and when I decided to take on this challenge, I was pretty scared. First, I wasn't a runner, as the most I had ever run was a couple of yards to catch a bus pulling off! Second, I didn't know how I was going to accomplish this, given that my level of fitness wasn't exactly where it needed to be to run 26.2 miles. Nevertheless, I did it!

When it comes to setting goals, an easy way to begin is by breaking down a large goal into smaller goals. By doing this, your goals will be much easier to accomplish. Smaller goals aren't so daunting or intimidating, so we tend to be able to work with them more effectively than with larger ones that seem insurmountable and intimidating. Whatever your goal may be, whether it's passing an upcoming test, finishing a project you have to turn in, or writing a business plan, rule number one is to set a completion date, and then break it down into smaller steps. **Here is an example from the marathon:**

1. Marathon date – March 4, 2007
2. Run 26.2 miles (I broke this down into two-mile increments, and every week I added two miles.)

Other examples:
English Test – 1 book to read; 14 chapters – Timeline: 2 weeks – 1 chapter a day
Bar Exam – 14 subjects to study – Timeline: 4 months – 3 to 4 subjects a month, 1 subject a week / 2-week revision of all subjects at end of timeline

23

Two miles feels a lot better and is a lot more palatable as a goal than 26.2 miles. Even saying two miles makes you breathe a little easier! If you don't break down your goals, inertia may set in, and you can easily lose your bearings. That is the simple reason a lot of people do not achieve the goals they set for themselves.

> "Champions know there are no shortcuts to the top. They climb the mountain one step at a time. They have no use for helicopters!"
> - Judi Adler

Now, you've broken down your goal into more palatable bite sizes. The next step is to create some kind of visual. A visual is a chart, a calendar, or something that you can actually see on a day-to-day basis and chart your progress. I use the LADDER, so that I can "Step it up!" one rung at a time.

The phrase "Step it up!" is also a motivator for me. I really want to be the best that I can be, so when I see my ladder, I realize that, in order to reach my goals and be the best that I can be, I have to step up my game! My ladder looks something like this:

At the top of the ladder, I write down the ultimate goal. Then on each rung of the ladder, I fill in all the smaller steps that are going to get me to the top of the ladder. In the case of the marathon, my six-month training period started in September 2006. I began to run an additional two miles at the end of each training week. So, for the period September to February, each rung reflected two more miles (Various rest periods were also taken into account.). The great thing about the ladder is that you can break it down into whatever small goals you're comfortable with. So, for example, if someone felt even the first two miles were too much, they could break it down further. It's really up to you. Once you break down your goals into more achievable bite sizes, you will feel relieved. Again, the reason I use a stepladder is because I'm reminded every day or every week that I need to literally "Step it up" to get where I need to go. Seeing the ladder every day adds some velocity behind my desire to reach those goals. As you complete each of the rungs, you can shade in that section of the ladder. Shading in the ladder is one of my favorite things to do; it's like getting that gold star in school. There is a great sense of accomplishment, and you start to want more gold stars!

> "We are not interested in the possibilities of defeat."
> — Victoria, Queen of England

It is all well and good to set goals; however, you also have to make a commitment to the larger goal at hand and to yourself. When I made the decision to run the marathon, I made a commitment to finish it, no matter what. It is amazing what happens when you commit to something, whether it is a task, a job, a business idea, or simply a concept. When you finally make the decision to commit, the world then starts laying gifts in front of you to help you achieve that goal, one after the other.

There is a great excerpt that I use for inspiration on commitment:

Until one is committed, there is always hesitancy,
the chance to draw back, always ineffectiveness.
Concerning all acts of initiative and creation
there is one elementary truth
the ignorance of which kills countless ideas
and splendid plans:
The moment one definitely commits oneself
then providence moves too.
All sorts of things occur to help one that would
never otherwise have occurred.
A whole stream of events issues from the decision
raising in one's favor all manner of
unforeseen incidents, meetings
and material assistance which no man
could have dreamed would come his way.
Whatever you can do, or dream you can do,
begin it.
Boldness has genius, power, and magic in it.
Begin it now.

- GOETHE

So, don't hesitate. Step up, step forward, declare your goal, create your ladder, and commit!

Now that you've committed to the larger goal at hand and you've started using the ladder technique, it is essential to put in place an accountability monitor. It's easy to cheat when no one is watching. If you're not the type that is generally self-motivated, this part of the equation is essential to the goal-setting process. If you are self-motivated, that is great—create your ladder and start working! My husband is my goal-setting partner. If you don't have a spouse, start this exercise with a friend, co-worker, or trusted business partner. It is best to obtain an accountability partner that you trust, someone that really believes in you and your goals. However, if you don't want to share your goals and ambitions with a friend, enlist the help of a coach. This is part of the equation that many people skip, because they believe they can handle it themselves, but it's amazing what an accountability partner can do for you and your goals. The objective here is for that person to make sure you are on track and that you are doing what you say you are going to do. Whether you check in with that person on a weekly or a monthly basis, the key is to make sure you set a time and stick with it.

This is a fun exercise to do with a friend. Set your goals separately, then exchange copies of your ladders and check in with each other weekly to ensure that you both are on task. Having an accountability partner does two things. First, it acts as a reporting mechanism. If you don't do what you say you're going to do and you end up having to give a bad report, you'll probably feel bad about your lack of progress. If you want to avoid this feeling, it will become an incentive for you to stick to the plan. Second, an accountability partner acts as a mirror of encouragement. If your partner is climbing up his or her ladder, it acts as a mirror and highlights what you should be doing, which can help give you the motivation you need.

Again, having this accountability monitor is one of the most important things you can do for yourself. It can be very hard to be motivated on your own at times. When you have someone watching you and helping you, it can certainly make a big difference.

"When someone you respect is watching and holding you accountable for your actions, it tends to bring out the best in everything you do…"
                                    – Erica Moore-Burton

Celebrate the Wins

Remember the concept that we discussed earlier: Success attracts Success. As you get used to success, make sure that you don't take it for granted. As I mentioned earlier, an important ingredient to goal setting and accomplishing goals is to always, always, always celebrate the wins. If you complete one rung on the ladder, reward yourself with something—perhaps a movie, a massage, or a walk in nature. You have to reward yourself, because that feeling of being rewarded can help you move to the next level of the ladder to "Step it up" to reach your ultimate goal.

Visualization

> "Envisioning the end is enough to put the means in motion."
> — Dorothea Brande

Another tool that I use very often is visualization. Visualization is seeing the end result in your mind. See yourself finishing that brief, being promoted, becoming a dentist, completing a successful presentation, practicing law, or crossing the finish line for a marathon—you name it. Many years ago, when I was taking the bar exam, I used the 'Step It Up' Ladder for my study plan. I had committed to taking the exam, had my visual ladder in front of me, and every day I would shade in a rung, and celebrate at the end of my studies with an episode of Seinfeld or Friends. It took me two attempts to pass the bar. The first time, I never really visualized myself passing the exam and enjoying the feelings of what it would feel like to accomplish such a feat. I want to emphasize the importance of feelings here. Enjoying feelings of completion helps us tremendously, because it helps release an energy within us that essentially attracts success to us. The second time that I took the exam, I had learned about the power of visualization. Every day—yes, every day—before I started to study, I sat at my desk and closed my eyes. I visualized the day that the exam results would come out. I would be sitting in front of my computer at home and typing my name into the state bar database. Then, after a few moments, I would see my name appear on the screen, indicating that I had been successful. I could see myself smiling from ear to ear. As I visualized this scenario, I felt the feelings of elation. Well, months later, exactly how I visualized receiving the results became a reality.

> "Man can only receive what he sees himself receiving."
> — **Florence Scovel Shinn**

Goal Setting For the Years Ahead

> "If we could only give, just once, the same amount of reflection to what we want to get out of life that we give to the question of what to do with a two weeks' vacation, we would be startled at our false standards and the aimless procession of our busy days." — **Dorothy Canfield Fisher**

If you ask ten of your closest friends where they want to be a year from now, five years from now, and ten years from now, I can almost guarantee you more than 50 percent of them may not have an answer. If they do have an answer, more than 80 percent of them will not have written it down. More often than not, when I coach people and ask them about their goals, they don't have anything written down. How can you climb up the stepladder if you don't know what it's leaning against? How can you create a road map when you don't know where you are going? It's like going on a journey without a clear destination in mind! This is the simple reason many people just wander through life, meandering from day to day without any clear vision. Have you ever met someone one year, and then run into them again five years later only to discover that they haven't really grown in any way? They are simply doing the same things they were doing when you first met them. I've found that those people are stuck in the same unproductive habits, surrounding themselves with the same kind of people and going through the same routines that aren't helping them to move forward. That is not conducive to growth. One thing that I have certainly found to be true is that as I get older, the years seem to go past faster and faster. Those who don't have a grasp on where they want to go and what they want to do in life are at risk of wasting years away. Planning for your future is imperative. Plans and desires can change, but when you have a road map, it makes life easier and more manageable.

> "You decide what it is you want to accomplish and then you lay out your plans to get there, and then you just do it. It's pretty straight forward."
> — **Nancy Ditz**

Start Today

Start today with these exercises. If you don't have time right now, make an appointment with yourself and write down that appointment date and time in your diary. Just like you would not miss an appointment to meet your best friend, don't miss this important appointment with yourself. After all, it's your future at stake. Set aside this time to think about your goals and write down what you want your life to look like one year from today, five years from today, and then ten years from today. I have listed some helpful categories to get you started, but be creative, and add more of your own too. Also, set in motion the Step It Up Ladder with some of the goals in your life (both long term and short term). It's fun to do, and you'll find that the structure will really help you achieve your goals. Consistency in reviewing your goals will help you stay on track, so don't forget your accountability monitor!

1. What I want three months from now:

   Career:

   Finances:

   Family:

   Health/Wellness:

   Spirituality:

2. What I want one year from now:

   Career:

   Finances:

   Family:

   Health/Wellness:

   Spirituality:

3. What I want five years from now:

   Career:

   Finance:

   Family:

Health/Wellness:

Spirituality:

4. What I want ten years from now

Career:

Finance:

Family:

Health/Wellness:

Spirituality:

5. Today, I commit to the following goals and will enlist the Step It Up Ladder technique to help get me there, one rung at a time. For this list choose different goals with different ranges, i.e., something that you want to complete within one month, six months, one year, two years, and beyond. Remember, success attracts success, so you will want to set some smaller goals in motion so that this universal law can kick in sooner rather than later upon the completion of your short-term goals.

Goal 1

Goal 2

Goal 3

Goal 4

Goal 5

chapter 3

Support Systems

What do support systems have to do with success? Well, I can tell you that you absolutely need one in order to be successful. Remember back when you were a kid and you were in a race or participating in a game of baseball. Remember when your parents, teacher, or friends were cheering you on from the sidelines telling you that you could do it; that you could make it happen? How did that feel? It probably made you feel as though you could conquer the world, and you probably performed a little better because you had people cheering you on, who believed in you. In order to lead successful lives, we still need people around us who uplift our spirits, encourage us, and remind us of our potential!

"My friends have made the story of my life. In a thousand ways they have turned my limitations into beautiful privileges, and enabled me to walk serene and happy in the shadow cast by my deprivation."
— **Helen Keller**

Who Do You Surround Yourself With?

EXERCISE

Write a list of the five people you surround yourself with most
frequently. This may include your spouse, co-workers, or friends

1. _____

2. _____

3. _____

4. _____

5. _____

This exercise is sometimes very difficult for people, because the person they spend most of their time with could be a family member or a spouse. Nevertheless, this is one of the most important exercises that you can complete in this book. Once you have created your list, examine how you feel when you're around him or her. What is each person's general disposition when you share ideas or thoughts? Rank each of them on a scale of one to ten, with a one indicating that they don't make you feel that great or are perhaps a negative force and ten indicating that they uplift your spirit, make you feel supported, or make you want to conquer the world!

If any of them rank at a five or below, then you have some work to do. For those who have all five people in a range of eight, nine, or ten, that is great. Keep surrounding yourself with those people. For those who rank seven or below, the next step is to examine why you feel this way around them. It could be that they are not supportive of your dreams and ideas, they are selfish and perhaps drain your energy so you have nothing left for yourself, or are simply always complaining about one thing or another. Whatever it is, really see if you can articulate why you feel that way. Remember, successful people surround themselves with other people who are successful. After you have established the reasons, make steps to spend less time with these people, or communicate your thoughts with them. Even go as far as to tell them about this exercise in this book! Also, consider whether you are the individual in the office that is surrounded by or is part of a group that is constantly complaining and gossiping, or whether you are in the group that is infused with positive energy, brainstorming about new ideas, and planning how to improve systems, productivity etc. It makes a big difference to your level of success when you are in the latter group.

"You will find yourself refreshed by the presence of cheerful people. Why not make an earnest effort to confer that pleasure on others? Half the battle is gained if you never allow yourself to say anything gloomy." **- Lydia M. Child**

Many years ago, I had a friend in my life who I really enjoyed being around. Let's call her Elizabeth. Liz was funny, smart, and outgoing. However, there were times when she just didn't make me feel good about myself. She would always critique my clothing, put down people I cared about, and try to embarrass me in front of others by making unpleasant jokes. All of this was done in a very surreptitious manner. I would always leave Liz feeling that I had had somewhat of a good time but not feeling that great about myself. Whenever I would share information about a project I was working on, she would always give me 1001 reasons why it probably wouldn't work. Again, this was all done with a smile on her face. I finally came to the realization that the relationship wasn't working for me.

Think about this as you consider all of those people that received a five or below in your exercise. This is the tough part where decisions have to be made. I mentioned that you have some work to do with these types of people in your life. I recommend these three productive courses of action:

1. Speak directly, frankly, and honestly with them about how you feel when you are around them.
2. Remove yourself completely from the situation and from their lives.
3. Maintain the relationships at a distance.

After doing this exercise many years ago, I found that there were three people who had a ranking of five or less and that I had to take appropriate action with each of them. After doing so, my life changed dramatically and for the better. Think about this: if you were Madonna (or any other artist), singing on stage, and you had some fans in the front row booing, laughing, and hissing. How do you think you would perform? Don't you think that you would perform better and with more confidence and gusto if the fans in the front row were cheering you on? Well, the same is true for your life. You will enjoy more success if you have a fan squad cheering you on every step of the way. Now, I am not suggesting that you want people around who aren't going to be honest with you and succumb to your every beck and call, but I am suggesting that the relationships you have should be examined very carefully and adjusted if necessary. Constructive, honest, uplifting, supportive relationships are the ones that will help you to be successful.

As to the individual I spoke about earlier, I confronted her very directly about how I felt when I was around her. After many months, when the situation didn't change, I removed myself completely from the situation and decided that I no longer could have her in my life. I can't tell you what a difference it makes in your life to have a great support system around you. When people around you believe that you can do anything, and you do too, guess what starts to happen? You start stepping up and living up to those expectations.

For any of those individuals who rank five or lower on your list, make a plan today to take action. Set a date to speak with him or her, remove yourself completely from the relationship, or start seeing or speaking less to that person and maintaining the relationship at a distance. When you start to communicate from a distance, it doesn't mean that you don't care about the person, it just means that you're not allowing that person's energy to infiltrate your life in a negative way.

> "Tell me whom you frequent, and I will tell you who you are."
>
> — French proverb

Fly With The Eagles
The Secret to Increasing Your Income

Many people have asked me, "What are some ways that I can raise my income?" Well, of course there is setting goals, making a plan and sticking to it, but there's more. It's as easy as surrounding yourself with people who are in the income bracket you want to be in. Your income is probably about the same—or within 20 percent—of the people you associate with most. Why would it be the same? Have you ever heard of the phrase "birds of a feather flock together"? They flock together because they are comfortable together; they generally share the same beliefs, go to the same places, and generally do the same types of things in life. Just like different cultures do different things, eat different types of food, wear different types of clothes, and have different overarching ideas about life, people in different income brackets share different ideas and attitudes. Do you think that the person who is making over $100,000 a year is doing the same things or having the same conversations as the person making $35.000? Is the person making $500,000 a year, doing the same things or having the same conversations as the person making $100,00? They certainly are not, and that is one thing of which I am certain. When you surround yourself with people in a higher income bracket, you start to learn and see things from a different perspective. You start to see patterns in how people generally live and behave, and I'm not just talking about their purchasing power. I'm talking about their habits as it relates to their work ethic, the books and magazines they read, the places they tend to go, the conversations they have on a daily basis, their day-to-day mindset, and the people they surround themselves with. The company you keep is such an important component for success. If you want to be a hair stylist, don't you think that it would benefit you to be around other hair stylists, so you can learn from them? We'll go into this a bit more later when we discuss mentors and obtaining the knowledge you need to get to where you want to go. The point here is simple: Associate with eagles until you grow your wings and become one.

"Surrounding yourself with dwarfs doesn't make you a giant."

— **Yiddish proverb**

Your Biggest Fan

It's all well and good to have a great support system in place, cheering you on from the sidelines and telling you that you can do it, but your biggest fan has to be you. If you don't believe that you can be successful in your mind, you probably won't be. You have to believe that you are deserving of success. Lack of belief and faith in yourself could derive from low self-esteem. So how can you build your confidence? We talked a little earlier about affirmations, and they will help; but, also you can look after yourself on a day-to-day basis so that you generally feel better about yourself. Are you getting enough sleep and exercise, and are you treating yourself to nice things? (Nice things don't necessarily have to cost a lot of money; they can be as simple and free as a walk on the beach, a candle lit hot bath, or a nice meal.) The other great way to help increase your self-esteem is to create a list of ten things that you like about yourself. On my list, I have things like my eyes, my sense of humor, the two little dimples on my face, the fact that I'm a loyal friend, and my generosity. Your list can be longer, but start with ten. Whenever you feel your confidence waning, take out your list and review the great things about yourself. Remind yourself that you are awesome!

Another nice exercise is to ask people around you (remember to ask the ones that you graded eight, nine, or ten!) to create a list of things they like about you. When I conducted self-esteem classes for young women a few years back, one of my favorite exercises was the "Confidence Builder." The participants wrote their names at the top of a blank piece of paper and then handed the paper to the girl next to them. At the bottom of the piece of paper that individual would write something that they liked about the person whose name was at the top.

After each girl was finished, she would fold the paper over to cover the comment. The piece of paper then went around the circle with the next person writing what they liked about the named person and folding the paper again covering the comment. This went on until the piece of paper was returned to the owner, and the only thing she could see was her name at the top. After we took a moment to recognize how it felt to pay other people genuine and heartfelt compliments, each participant would slowly unfold the piece of paper and read the comments that others had said about her. It was great to see their faces as they read all the comments—some of the compliments they had never heard, and others hadn't considered themselves to possess certain traits before the exercise. Many years later, I got an e-mail from one of the young women who had kept that piece of paper and told me that she read that piece of paper every day through a difficult period in her life as a reminder that she was worthy of happiness.

Whatever you need to do to keep and maintain a healthy self-esteem, do it. Everyone has shortcomings, things they don't like about themselves, and areas in their lives that they feel need improvement. Remember that no one is exempt, not even the celebrities that you read about. However, maintaining a high self-esteem requires an investment of your time. It's something that you have to keep working on. Just like you look after your hair or your nails, your self-esteem needs time and attention. Give it the attention it deserves, because when you pay attention to it, the world within you changes and the world outside changes its response to you.

> "I've learned to take time for myself and to treat myself with a great deal of love and respect 'cause I like me … I think I'm kind of cool."
>
> – Whoopi Goldberg

LOVING ME EXERCISE
Start now by making a list of things you like about yourself, and
review your list daily for the next week:

1. _____

2. _____

3. _____

4. _____

5. _____

6. _____

7. _____

8. _____

9. _____

10. _____

How Do You Treat Others?

People make the world go around, and I often recount the
motto about treating people the way you would like to be
treated. As you will read throughout this little book, in
order to be successful you need other people. No woman
is an island. I don't care how successful someone is, it
has taken the help of many people for her to get where
she is. Take Oprah for example. Do you think Harpo (her
production company) would be as successful without
the input, hard work, and diligence of thousands and
thousands of people? My mother told me something
when I was very young that resonated well into my adult
years and still does today. It was that you should always
treat people well as you go up the ladder in life, because
you don't know who you're going to pass on the way down.

41

This essentially means that if, for some reason, you should take a fall as you go up the ladder of life, there may or may not be helping hands available. This, of course, will depend on how you treated people along the way. Now, of course that shouldn't be the only reason you treat people well—we all want to be treated with respect and dignity on our journey, and no journey is more important than the next—but it is something to consider.

> "I shall not pass this way again: then let me now relieve some pain, remove some barrier from the road, or brighten someone's heavy load."
>
> – Eva Rose Park

In my life, I have met some very arrogant people who have felt that because they attained a certain level of education, or made a certain amount of money they deserved to be treated "differently," with more respect, reverence, and adoration than others. Everyone is on a different journey in life. Consider the waitress at your local coffee shop, who too has worked really hard to get where she is and to make the amount that she is making, who works really hard on the job to ensure that everyone is being served coffee exactly to his or her liking on a daily basis and with a smile. Then, consider the high-flying attorney with two advanced degrees, making a six-figure income, who works hard to help individuals with their labor and employment issues. What is the difference between the two? They have both worked hard to get where they are in life; they both wake up every day to do their jobs to the best of their ability; and they both are serving in one way or another. The difference may be that one person is working in a plush high-rise building in the middle of a city and sitting in a corner office, while the other is behind a counter in a busy pedestrian area. The difference is in the pay checks they receive at the end of the day. The difference may be that one had the ability, capacity and opportunity to obtain a formal education. And, obviously, the difference is in the type of work and the skill level needed for each type of position. However, take a moment to look at the foundation, or the essence of what each person is doing on a daily basis—working for a living, serving others, getting up each day, being productive and contributing to society. When you look at it in those terms, why should either be treated differently, and what does it cost to treat other people with respect because of the service they are providing?

> "My satisfaction comes from my commitment to advancing a better world."
>
> - Faye Wattleton

When was the last time someone treated you unkindly or didn't give you the respect you felt you deserved? How did that feel? I would imagine that it didn't feel very good at all. I have encountered hundreds of people who are really rude to sales people who call them at home to try to sell a product or a service that they aren't interested in. If you're one of those individuals, the next time you receive a sales call, try smiling to yourself and responding with a polite, "No thanks, I'm not really interested at the moment but have a great day, and thank you for calling." You will have done two things by using this approach: First, you have declined politely using a different technique that doesn't leave you feeling stressed and irritated. Second, you will have treated the person on the other end of the line with dignity and respect—the way I suspect you would wish to be treated. Telemarketing is one of the most challenging jobs out there, because a lot of the people who receive sales calls are not only rude and obnoxious, but also simply hang up. Imagine in your business—whether you are an executive, a lawyer, a doctor, or a business owner—how you would feel if every time you called someone else in your office (your manager, a customer, or a co-worker) they were rude to you, hung up on you, or bombarded you with a few choice expletives. How would you feel? Do you think someone who is in a higher position than you—your manager, your co-worker, or your customer—should treat you with any less respect than they treat their peers? The world seems very different when you think about it in those terms, doesn't it?

> "In this life, we must help each other to the best of our ability. We all have a different gift to share. One is not better than the other, it just is."
>
> – Erica Moore-Burton

I use the example above for many reasons. I am a big believer that, as human beings, we simply should maintain a decent level of respect among us. It costs nothing to treat others with respect. There isn't a high price tag associated with it. Every time you treat someone with respect, it doesn't take anything away from you; it only adds richness to your character. I have a couple of short stories to share with you that exemplify a few repercussions of treating others badly.

I was once working with a job seeker (we call them candidates in the recruiting field) who was a successful junior lawyer (they are called Associates). I had been working with her for about four months when I sent her on an interview with one of my clients who was looking for someone with her exact credentials. I just knew that they would fall in love with each other, and it would be a perfect fit. I spent countless hours coaching her on what to wear for the interview, what questions to ask, research

44

on the firm, and responses to inevitable questions. As I waited patiently in my office for her to call after the interview, a few hours passed. Finally, the phone rang. The conversation went a little something like this:

"So, how was it?"

"Erica, it was amazing. Thank you so much for setting this up for me. I really liked Tom, and I met with three of his partners, who were equally as impressive. They asked all the questions you thought they would, and I answered all of them as we planned. I really think they're going to make me an offer."

Well, of course I was ecstatic to hear that. The next step was to hear back from the client to confirm the feeling was mutual. A few hours later, I did receive a call from the firm. However, that conversation was very different:

"Hi Tom. So, Sarah came in today. I heard that it went very well from her end. What were your thoughts?"

Tom sighed. "Well, Erica, to be honest with you, I thought she was quite impressive on paper. She seems to be really smart, and had all the credentials that we are looking for."

"Great, that's great," I responded, but I could hear the BUT coming.
After a moment's silence, it did.

"But, Erica ... we're going to pass on this occasion."

"Really? I'm confused. You said that it seems like she has everything you were looking for. Was there something missing?"
"Yes, I'm afraid so."

"Can I ask what?"

"Sure. Well, you see, our receptionist is my niece, and she is an integral part of the team here. She's really the glue of the firm, and we're actually training her for an office manager position. She's that good."

"Go on," I pressed.

"Well, we usually get my niece to do a little pre-screening for us, you know, just engage our prospective employees in a little conversation, and I'm afraid Sarah didn't pass that test."

"Really?"

"Yes, and before you say it, I do give them the benefit of the doubt - nerves, etc., but on the way out after a great interview she validated her parking, gave her a bottle of water, and her attitude wasn't much different. I don't even think she got so much as a thank you. I just can't have those types working at the firm, I'm afraid. Good interpersonal skills are an integral part of this job, and we're all a team here."

I was shocked, to say the least. After a lot of probing with Sarah (and the actual receptionist), I discovered that Sarah hadn't made any eye contact with the receptionist, had picked up a magazine as she waited, and she didn't even look up as the receptionist tried to make conversation. When Sarah was offered water, she didn't seem to appreciate the gesture, and didn't say thank you as she left after they paid for her parking.

Unfortunately, there have been many Sarahs that have lost positions because of the way they've treated people who they perceived to be lower on the totem pole. The

46

lack of a few cordial words cost Sarah a six-figure salary and a position with a prestigious law firm in the Los Angeles area.

The second story is that of a friend of mine, Tony, who was involved in a relationship with a woman who he seemed to be quite fond of. He had been dating her for a while, but there was one thing that was niggling at him, something that was preventing him from getting more serious with her. When I probed a little more, I found out that she treated him like a king, but when it came to other people and her family, the story wasn't the same. She wasn't polite to waiters at restaurants, administrative assistants, cleaners at her office, some family members, and other people that she believed hadn't achieved the same level of success as she had. For him, it was a real turnoff. He broke up with her a few months later. Many years later, he ran into her and the issue hadn't really subsided from what he could tell. Although she was doing well in her career, she hadn't found that special person with whom to share her life. He had a strong suspicion that her attitude and lack of respect for others had something to do with it.

chapter 4

Relationships

Excellent relationships are an important component of success. During one of my coaching sessions, I met Lisa. Lisa was a bright, charismatic, and successful woman who wanted to transition from one job to another. As I sat down with her to get to know her a little better, we talked about some of her relationships and her network. I discovered that Lisa didn't have many friends. At the time, she wasn't talking to her mother or her sister, and she didn't have a strong professional network. She was having difficulty trying to make a transition, and I could clearly see one of the reasons she was having a hard time. All of her relationships were in tatters. She hadn't spent the time over the years to invest in anyone in her life or professional network, because she didn't feel the need to, and because she had reached a certain level of success.

Relationships are about investing not only in other people, but also in yourself. Remember that cheering squad we talked about earlier? Even if you are the most self-motivated person, eventually you will need someone else's help. Therefore, it is imperative to invest time nurturing and developing strong relationships. Things get done through relationships—jobs are found, employees are developed, deals are made, and advice is given and received. The list goes on and on, and it's all done through relationships. With Lisa, we began by making a list of the relationships that weren't in good shape. Then, we started with an action plan to repair certain relationships that were affecting her life, because of unresolved issues. Finally, we started to work on developing some new relationships. With some of her relationships, nothing detrimental had happened; she had just lost touch as she started to develop and move ahead in her career. With her mother, a rift had developed, because she stopped calling as much as the years went on, and she hadn't seen her mother in about two years, even though she lived only two hours away. Did you know that one of the biggest regrets for many people later in life is that they wish they had spent less time working and more time on their relationships? Here are some tips I shared with Lisa to help her nurture her relationships.

❚ Reach out to those individuals you haven't spoken with in some time with a phone call, and set a reminder in your calendar to do so every couple of months.

❚ Take the time to visit friends and family, no matter how busy you are, and include this as part of your schedule at the beginning of the month or year.

❚ Invite a group of friends that you are out of touch with to a restaurant for a group dinner. Then, follow up with each of them individually for a coffee date or a phone call within a month. You may find that some of your friends have things in common. Then you could schedule group events with one or more individuals more frequently to help maintain the relationships.

❚ Send a handwritten note to those friends who are too far away to meet with personally, but who you have been out of contact with for a while.

Those were just a few starting points we used to get some of Lisa's relationships back on track.

"I'd like people to think of me as someone who cares about them."
                                     - Diana, Princess of Wales

Networking

For those of you who are eager to climb the career ladder, networking is one of the best things you can do. Lisa hadn't built a network, because she felt she didn't need one. She had been in a secure position and didn't really need other people to do her job. However, when it was time for her to move and find a new career, she didn't have a network that she could tap into. Therefore, building a network was another area that I worked on with Lisa. Networking can open up so many doors for you, and it was eventually through networking that Lisa actually landed her next position with the company she desired. We set in place an action plan for her to attend a minimum of three networking events per month. We found suitable events through the Internet and other local publications. The prospect of going to any networking events was initially very daunting for Lisa, but we worked on ways she could work the room, conversational approaches she could take, and follow-up techniques.

Five-Step Networking Exercise

▌ Check the Internet and locate a minimum of three networking events that you can attend this month. Commit to attending them with a friend or colleague. Check out Meetup.com or your local business periodical online for listings.
▌ When you attend your first networking event, commit to meeting three new people and obtaining their business cards. Write something on the back of their cards that will remind you of who they are, perhaps something you spoke about or a personal interest that they discussed.
▌ Follow up with each person with a handwritten note,

e-mail, or phone call and tell them it was nice to meet them and that you would like to stay in touch.

■ The next time you hear about a networking event, an interesting piece of news, or a personal professional update, e-mail those individuals and let them know about it!

■ If time permits, schedule a coffee, lunch or dinner meeting with your new professional contacts from time to time.

> "Each friend represents a world in us, a world not possibly born until they arrive, and it is only by this meeting that a new world is born."
>
> **- Anais Nin**

Kindness Begets Kindness

Contemplate the following:

1. When was the last time you over tipped a waiter or waitress?
2. When was the last time you took the time to have a real conversation with someone in a service role?
3. When was the last time you let someone in front of you while driving?
4. When was the last time you thanked someone from your past for the influence or effect they had on you or your life?
5. When was the last time you brought a gift for a friend just because?

Do something kind for another person every day for the next seven days in a row. When you give generously to the world, it gives back generously to you.

chapter 5

Visibility

Many people have asked me over the years how I managed to get promotions quickly and seemingly so easily while working in corporate America. There are a number of factors that contributed to my success, but one of the important ones was making myself highly visible. No matter where you are on the career ladder, in order to get from one rung to the next you have to be highly visible— highly visible to yourself and those around you. We're going to explore the concept of visibility in this chapter, so that you can start putting it into practice immediately and see the results.

Visibility of Self

Visibility of self speaks directly to self-awareness. In order to be successful you need to have a keen awareness of who you are, what you stand for, and what your talents are. As we said earlier, this is a process that will take more than ten minutes to complete. For some people, it takes a lifetime; for others, spending an hour a day or hours a week really delving into the nuts and bolts of their makeup has propelled them to levels of unimaginable success. It's akin to being a pilot on an airplane; the pilot has to know where he is going in order to operate and navigate the plane to the final destination. He knows the intricacies of the plane, how it works, the altitude at which to fly, and what to do in emergency situations. Let's use the plane as a symbol for our lives. How many of us are simply passengers, letting someone else dictate to us rather than getting in the pilot's seat and really directing our own lives to where we want to go? Taking the time to get to know yourself on many different levels is essential to guide your plane through life. The first person you need to become visible to is yourself. At times, this can be a painful process, because part of being visible is examining the good and the bad, your weaknesses and your strengths. Once you have been able to conduct a thorough assessment, it's time to let your light shine and create the visibility that is needed to take yourself to the next level. This can be a challenging concept for some people who find it difficult to promote themselves, but there are many techniques you can undertake to make this happen. It's all well and good to have great talent and skills, but if no one really knows about them, how can you get ahead?

Imagine if Beyonce just kept her talent and her voice to herself, and sang and danced in front of the mirror in her bathroom every single day. Do you think that she would be where she is today? It's the same with your job and career. First things first, below I have detailed ten questions to help get you started on a basic self-assessment. Take approximately 5 to 10 minutes to finish each sentence, and it will help you examine your thoughts in greater depth.

1. My strongest three skills are ...
2. My family and friends know me for ...
3. My family and friends can rely on me for ...
4. I am always complimented for ...
5. I need to improve on my ...
6. I have been commended in the past for ...
7. I am comfortable with ...
8. I am uncomfortable with ...
9. My greatest weakness is ...
10. My strongest desire right now is to ...
11. I stand for ...
12. I love my...

Start by answering these questions, by doing so you can gain some clarity about who you are, what you're good at, what your natural talents are, and the areas in which you need to improve.

> "I think self-awareness is probably the most important thing towards becoming a champion."
>
> **- Billie Jean King**

For those of you who feel stuck and for some reason feel as though you just can't get ahead, make sure you complete all the exercises in this book. You truly need to have a strong sense of yourself before you become visible to others. At the end of the day, if you become visible for the wrong attributes, it can be a hindrance and present obstacles instead of helping you propel to new heights.

Visible To Others
Asking For What You Want

I obtained my first management position by asking for it. However, I didn't ask for it before I had made myself visible. Making yourself visible to others is about stepping into roles before they actually become yours. This about "acting the part." Perhaps a good way to start is by taking the initiative and going the extra mile on projects that have been assigned to you. Before I became a manager, I created a plan. My plan was to observe other successful managers around me. How did they act? Did people respect them, and if so, why? If not, why not? What did they do on a day-to-day basis? What did I observe about their work ethic? How did they speak to others, and how did they dress? Months before I felt as though I was ready for the role, I started to emulate the people I admired in my own role. Remember, I wasn't a manager, but I started to conduct myself like one. What I was doing was stepping into the role. I started carrying myself differently, and I started teaching others about what I knew by conducting short training programs for new hires at the company. I started speaking up in meetings with ideas that I had fleshed out and thought about ahead of time. I started volunteering to do things other people didn't want to do. I even made sure that I was one of the best dressed women in the office by making a further investment in my wardrobe. I started doing all of these "extra" things while performing at a very high level in my own position. I made sure not to step on any toes with the current management team, but instead helped them in their roles. I also started to befriend and ask questions of other trusted managers in other departments and making notes about what their responsibilities were. I studied their paths and what they had done to get to where they were. On a day-to-day basis, I simply played the part.

Do you know what happens when you start to play the part? When you start to play the part, people start to see you as that person, and start to interact and react to you very differently. As I started to play the part, newer people coming into the company, as well as existing employees, started treating me differently. They started to treat me like a manager. I was the one that they turned to with problems when managers weren't around because I was always willing to help. I was the one they asked to act as a mentor to them. I started to learn more about the ins and outs of the department, so people came to rely on me as a trusted source of information. About a year later, one of the managers unexpectedly decided to leave the company after being there for many years. Have you heard of the phrase, "Luck is when preparedness meets opportunity"? Well, I had been preparing myself for this role, because this was what I wanted as my next step. At the time, the company considered hiring an experienced manager to take the role. That was when I stepped up to the plate and asked for the position. Sometimes in life you have to ask for what you want and, more important, be who you want to be before you actually are that person. Of course, I was met with many objections at first. The biggest objection was that I didn't have any previous management experience. The management team asked me to write a memo on what it meant to be a good manager and why I felt that I could be that person. Well, I had mentors; I had been studying leadership at home, and I had been playing the part for many months. Therefore, it was very easy for me to write a compelling piece on the traits of a good manager. After a series of interviews, which included questions that I could easily answer, because I had been asking other managers questions about their experiences over a long period of time, the role was awarded to me.

I tell this story not to brag, but to highlight a few things that you can put into practice today. Regardless of where you are in your career—whether you are already working in corporate America, or whether you own your own business—stepping up to the next level of success can naturally occur by simply taking on the role. Play bigger than you actually are at this time, and you will naturally start to fill those shoes.

> "Women who are confident of their abilities are more likely to succeed than those who lack confidence, even though the latter may be much more competent and talented and industrious.'"
>
> **- Dr. Joyce Brothers**

If you are an assistant and you have strong organizational skills and a desire to step into a managerial/supervisory role, get creative and start to take on bigger projects or even projects that are outside the scope of your current position. Could you organize a company picnic or a charity event on behalf of the company? Could you arrange for a speaker to come into your organization and speak to the group and obtain a sponsor at the same time? Think big when it comes to creating visibility. Obviously, going from an assistant position to a director position isn't going to happen overnight. There is going to be some work to do and this may include further education. Promotions aren't out of the realm of possibility. You could take more responsibility within your current role with an increase in salary. There are many success stories about people starting off in the mail rooms of large organizations and many years later heading large departments. It's like creating a public relations campaign for yourself. If celebrities don't have good public relations teams surrounding them, they can find it hard to get ahead, because eventually they will be forgotten. Note that it is possible to create negative PR as well. Make sure that you're on the right side of the coin.

> "The thing women have got to learn is that nobody gives you power. You just take it."
>
> **- Roseanne**

One of my clients, Melanie, worked for a customer service department. Although she liked the day-to-day duties in her position, she felt she wasn't being challenged enough. We established that some of her talents incorporated teaching and educating other people. She was doing it over the phone in her daily routine, but not in a way that challenged her. We created a plan for her to start speaking up about some of her ideas in company training sessions and detailing some of her novel ideas. Instead of just "showing up" for training sessions, she actually started preparing for them, so she could present some of her ideas at appropriate times. After about six months of creating that visibility, we discussed ways in which she could start approaching her management team with a proposal for an ongoing monthly training program that she would conduct. It was not something that interfered with the company's objectives but, in fact, enhanced them. It was also a program that would be fun for the other customer service representatives: on a monthly basis, they could talk about the challenges they faced and ways in which they could improve their service. It was also devised as a voluntary program. After a review of her proposal, Melanie's idea was implemented about six to seven months later, and with great success. Every month, Melanie's program was filled, because the other customer service representatives felt that she was adding value and information to their roles. Less than a year later, she was promoted into a division manager role.

If you're a business owner, the same things can happen for you. Customers buy products and services that can add value to their lives; it's as simple as that. What value are you adding, and how are you articulating that at every opportunity? Creating visibility is essential for business owners, but what more can you do to create a buzz surrounding your product or service in your community? Can you tell stories about your customers and how your products or services have enhanced their lives? Can you publish articles, talk to local groups, or create a buzz about your expertise in selling your product/service? Again, even if you're not a full expert, step into the role and become one. By learning, acting, and fully embodying what you want to be, you can create it for yourself.

QUESTIONS

1. What do I ultimately want from my career?
2. What five things can I do today to step into that role?
3. What five questions can I ask someone else who is in a role that I would like to be in?
4. I commit to answering these questions by

_____

(no more than seven days after of reading this).

Sign here: _____

"Never bend your head. Hold it high.
Look the world straight in the eye."
                                        - Helen Keller

chapter **6**

Becoming an Expert

Regardless of whether you're a hair stylist, junior auditor, executive assistant, or C-level executive at a Fortune 1000 company, the road to success contains the same basic elements and a high level of commitment. Many people look at successful people and think that they just arrived easily at their current level of success. They do not see the hours of study, preparation, work, risk, or effort that went into getting to that level. That preparation takes effort and commitment. I have a friend, let's call her Janet, who is quite an accomplished actress and has been in many popular shows. She wanted to be an actress from the age of 18 and spent many years studying and acting in theaters where at times only two people would show up to see her perform. She faced rejection after rejection when she auditioned for roles. She did have some small successes along the way, which essentially kept her going. One thing she always did was keep her eyes on the prize. Eleven years later, yes, 11 years later, she landed a role on a national television show that took her career to new heights. Every magazine in town wanted to take her picture, wanted to know who she was dating, what she was wearing, what she ate and many organizations invited her to host national events. The people that didn't know her well before she landed the television show didn't see all the years of effort that she had put in, the closed doors that she had to face, and the risks that she had to take to get to where she was. She didn't just walk into the audition room for the show and land the role without a substantial amount of effort, work, and commitment. Essentially she had spent close to eleven years preparing, learning, and perfecting her craft so that when the opportunity came along, she was ready.

"The dedicated life is the life worth living."
- Annie Dillard

It takes time to become recognized as an expert. You don't just wake up one day and call yourself an expert. It can take many months, in most cases years, to be deemed an expert in a   given task, field, or industry. When individuals are recognized as experts, many opportunities open up for them. These opportunities can be promotions, new projects, exposure to different people, interesting ventures—the list goes on and on.

How do you become an expert?

In terms of career growth and development, you become an expert by simply being knowledgeable about your given role, profession or skill. The definition of expert is:

"A person who has special skill or knowledge in some particular field."

Being an expert requires some level of commitment and stick-to-itiveness. I have known many individuals who tend to jump from job to job every six months, never sticking with any one thing long enough to become very good at anything, much less an expert. It can be difficult to create traction or any kind of momentum when you are continually jumping from one role to another.   However, bear in mind that it is definitely a different thing to jump from one project to another, if you are expanding on what you've done on previous projects.

Becoming an expert is kind of like building a house. A strong foundation needs to be established; then you can continue to build upon it. Becoming an expert means that you have learned and continue to learn about that given

62

task, role, industry, profession, product, or service, and you essentially know an extraordinary amount about it. If a layperson asked you a question about that given task, role, industry, profession, product, or service, you would be able to give them detailed and expert information about it. Wherever you are on the career ladder, don't underestimate the power of becoming an expert, whether it is on a particular computer program, a particular transaction or a specific procedure. In fact, you can become an expert on anything you like!

Continued Learning

"It is with enterprises as with striking fire; we do not meet with success except with reiterated efforts."

- Francoise d'Aubigne

I personally set a target for the number of books that I am going to read in any given year, and I keep track of those books. I read a minimum of two books per month, as well as listen to audiotapes in my car and read my regular magazine and newspaper subscriptions. I read every day, even if I can read only a couple of pages. I am continually learning something new about self-development and growth. This provides me with new information that I can share in my seminars, methods to enhance my coaching programs and most important my own personal growth and development. They have something called continuing legal education (CLE) credits in the legal field, and every lawyer is required to complete a certain number of continuing education courses within a given year. It's not enough to have gone through law school and have passed the bar exam; in order to keep your license active you are required to complete these courses to get the credit. Why do you think the profession is set up this way? Well, simply so that lawyers stay abreast of changes in the law and keep their knowledge current. Well, the same concept should be applied to whatever profession you're in, regardless of whether it is "required." Continued learning is something that you have to be motivated to do for your career growth and development. You have to keep learning about your profession. It's what makes the great, great while others sit on the sidelines wondering what the secret to success is.

> "Success depends in a very large measure upon individual initiative and exertion, and cannot be achieved except by a dint of hard work."
> **- Anna Pavlova**

If you read a minimum of 30 minutes to 1 hour per day every day on your chosen subject, you will become an expert in 4 to 5 years. Another way to assimilate knowledge and to make it stick, is to teach others what you are learning along the way.

Remember, you don't just arrive at success without doing the work to get there. And just because you arrived at your definition of success doesn't necessarily mean that you are going to maintain it. You have to continually grow. We've all seen those celebrities who attain a certain level of success, and then are nowhere to be seen a few years later. Similarly, consider the executive who has climbed to the top of her organization. That executive won't stay there unless she continues to obtain successful results. Just because someone "arrives" doesn't mean that the work, growth, and development has to stop. In fact, it must continue for the executive to either stay in her current position or get to the next level. By becoming an expert and making a commitment to stay an expert, you can pretty much ensure your own success.

"Elbow grease is the best polish."

- English proverb

Take Expert Action

Absolutely nothing happens without action. You may be thinking there are some great ideas in this book. Well, if you don't put any of them into practice, how can you improve or develop yourself? Remember the phrase, "Nothing happens without action." If you want to be an expert, declare it, learn about it, then be it!

To get you started, fill in the following:

1. I am going to become an expert in _____.

2. Within the next month, I am going to learn the following things about my role/profession/business.

3. Who do I know that is an expert in this field?

If possible, make an appointment to meet with this person to learn more. Or, if the person is famous, read about his or her life in an autobiography or watch a documentary about his or her life.

chapter 7

Knowledge Is Power

I didn't realize the power of having a mentor until I was well into my twenties. Once I experienced what a mentor could help me accomplish, I haven't been without one since. Did you know that even the most successful people have mentors and coaches? Oprah Winfrey has mentors and coaches. Lisa Nichols has a spiritual mentor, a financial coach, and several other mentors who she talks to regularly about her career and life direction?

So, what is the purpose of a mentor? A mentor can help guide you when making life and career decisions. He or she can show you different perspectives, give you tips and advice, and guide you to resources that can help you navigate your journey. You have to choose your mentors carefully and wisely, though. You want individuals you trust implicitly, because the goal is for you to be completely open and honest with them so that they can steer you in the right direction.

My early mentors were individuals who I would reach out to and speak with occasionally. I have also had mentors with whom I have set up regular weekly or monthly appointments. When engaging the help of a mentor, remember to be respectful of his or her time. Set appointments that are convenient, and make sure that you stick to the allotted time you have predetermined. At the end of the day, most mentors will be helping you from the goodness of their own hearts, so you never want to monopolize their time.

Those climbing the career ladder ideally should choose a mentor who is a few steps or more ahead of them on the ladder. When I was a manager of a sales team in Los Angeles, I chose an individual who was a regional manager over several large branches on the West Coast as a mentor. It is important to choose someone that is further along than you, because one of the purposes of a mentor is to speak to you from experience. Ideally, you want someone who is more experienced than you, so that you can learn from their successes and failures, their good experiences and their bad ones. While it is important to choose someone who is ahead of you on the career ladder, it's also important that you respect that individual for his or her contributions. It's better to choose a mentor you respect and admire to get the most out of the relationship.

A mentor can help you stay on track and help you remain accountable for your actions. I used to get homework assignments from one of my mentors on a weekly basis; she would end each call with something for me to do for the following week. Well, I didn't ever want her to think that I was wasting her time and efforts, so I would ensure that anything she asked me to do was done in full by the time of our next call. Those assignments helped me grow tremendously, because I would have to put everything that we discussed into action by the following week. By the end of our mentoring sessions, I felt 100 percent more effective in my role.

How do you find a mentor? Most of my mentors have been people that I worked with. However, some were people that I read about or met in passing and asked them to be my mentors. Others have been business associates and friends. A mentor can really be anybody you choose. For me, it's been as simple as approaching them, sincerely complimenting them on their work or career achievements, telling them about my personal goals and objectives, and then asking them if they would be willing to mentor me on some level (whatever they were comfortable with in terms of their time commitment).   Some people are willing to have lunch for a one-time mentoring session while others are willing to mentor for extended periods. You have to ask for what you want and uncover what kind of relationship the individual is prepared to have. If a person says no, don't take it personally; respect their decision, and don't hold a grudge. Simply move on to ask the next person on your list. Remember, time is a precious commodity. Anyone you deem to be successful is probably very busy, so you have to be respectful of his or her time. Extend small, kind gestures: buy lunch for them, send a kind note from time to time, or give them a small gift as a token of your appreciation. Everybody feels good when they are recognized, and even a short note can go a very long way.

As I have stated, once you've found a mentor, the goal of the relationship is to learn from his or her experience. This can help you get where you want to go faster. Make sure that you are fully prepared for your mentoring sessions by having a list of questions prepared in advance. Of course, the mentor will need to know where you are in order to help you, so you may be responsible for much of the talking to start with, but be sure to squeeze in some pertinent questions, so that you can extract information that will ultimately help you up the ladder. Mentoring sessions are not the time to do a verbal dump about the problems of the day, people who irk you or other personal problems. This is the time to glean information, so you can strategically develop your plan for reaching your goals and becoming the person you wish to be.

Here are some questions that I have used in the past that can help you get started with your mentoring relationship. The key is to ask intelligent, insightful questions. I have even found that answering them has helped my mentors a great deal in their own lives!

1. How did you get started in this career?
2. What is the biggest mistake you've made in your career to date, and what did you do to correct it?
3. If you had the chance to do anything differently what would it be?
4. Who are your mentors?
5. What would be the most important piece of advice you would give to someone like me?
6. What was the best thing that you did for your career, and why?
7. What types of books and magazines do you read on a daily basis, and do you have any titles that you would recommend for me?
8. What are your goals for the next five/ten years?
9. Is there anyone else that you would recommend I speak with or learn about?
10. How do you set goals and what mechanisms do you use to achieve them?

"If we would have new knowledge, we must get a whole world of new questions."

- Susanne K. Langer

When I choose mentors, I always choose people that I know are the best at what they do. I want to know what has made that person successful. I want to know about their daily habits, work ethic, what they are reading daily and who they associate with. I also want to know about any articles that they may have written, and any awards they may have received. Never think that you're preparing too much or asking too many questions. At the end of the day, people love to talk about themselves, so it's a win-win situation all the way around.

70

Handling Challenges

"Your first big trouble can be a bonanza if you live through it. Get through the first trouble, and you'll probably make it through the next one."   **- Ruth Gordon**

Mentors can provide you with much-needed encouragement during challenging times. Everyone has them; nothing is smooth sailing all the way through life. A mentor can provide you with an objective opinion and guide you to greener pastures.

A note to remember is that you can have mentors for everything: your financial affairs, health and nutrition, career, and family life. Mentoring doesn't have to be associated with just your career. Help yourself by taking the shortcut and enlist the help of a mentor today.

Find A Mentor Exercise

1. Make a list of the people you know (and perhaps don't know) in your life today who could be a mentor to you.
2. Write a detailed description of the kind of mentor you would like.
3. Start asking your family, friends, and associates if they know anybody that fits this description.
4. Make a phone call, write a letter or a handwritten note to the individuals you have identified (or that others have recommended to you) as possible mentors. Ask them if they would be willing to either speak with you or meet with you to discuss a mentor/mentee relationship.

"No matter what accomplishments you make, somebody helped you."
                                              - Althea Gibson

From One Perspective To Another

I'll tell you a short story about a former colleague of mine who worked at the same law firm I did. Let's call her Sally.

Sally started her first day on the job as an Associate. When I first saw Sally, I was actually surprised the firm had hired her because of her appearance. She had scruffy hair, and her clothes looked as though they hadn't been ironed or dry-cleaned. She wore thick-rimmed glasses, and I surmised that she was probably really smart and had diminished eyesight from all the reading she had done in law school. Well, after Sally started talking, I found I was right about her being smart. Some people know a little about everything, but Sally was that person who knew a lot about a lot. She was an absolute genius in many people's minds. After the second week, I walked into her office to talk about a project that we would be working on together. As I walked through the door, I couldn't believe what I saw around me. On her desk were three empty bottles of Coke, one half-full bottle of Sprite, pretzels strewn all over the desk, empty chip packets on the floor, and paper strewn all over the office. This is not an exaggeration either! Her office was an absolute disaster. I have never seen anything like it in my life. Her office was in the most horrendous state that I had ever seen an office in my life. Well, first of all, I wasn't that enthralled about working with her on the project. My first thought was, "If this is the state of her office, what is the real state of her mind?" As we started to work on the project, important documents started to go missing. She couldn't locate pertinent reading materials, and a whole host of other things happened that made it very difficult for us to work together. We eventually got the project done, but her cleanliness and the state of her office space became worse and worse over the months. It got to a point where some of the attorneys in the office didn't want to work with her because of its condition. Sally had an issue: clearly, she was unable to keep an organized and clean space. Ultimately, she was let go from the firm for "performance-related issues." Her lack of organization and the excessive clutter in which she worked definitely had something to do with it. The chatter and stories about her among other employees continued for months after she was gone. Although Sally was very smart, one wouldn't have thought so because of the way she kept her surroundings. The natural progression of her career trajectory would have had her meet with clients. What client would want to do business with someone who couldn't keep her office space clean and organize herself first? Sometimes, the thing we need to face to take our lives to the next level is a personal flaw that is preventing us from doing so. Sally was let go and couldn't experience that next level of success at least not at that particular law firm.

My point in telling this story is that perception is everything, and sometimes we have foibles and flaws that others around us may just be accepting as part of who we are. Sally, in this case, was told in a roundabout way about the condition of her office–"performance-related issues." But, I could tell you countless other stories about individuals who can't seem to get ahead for one reason or another, and everyone around them knows the reason, except for them! If you have a flaw that is preventing you from reaching another level of success in your life–for example, the relationship you're looking for, the friendships you want, the promotion you've been wanting, or the business success you've been chasing—wouldn't you want to know about it? Sometimes we are lucky enough to have people in our lives who can tell us about some flaws that may be hindering us in certain areas of our lives. What you'll find is that most people don't even ask! When was the last time you asked someone what they thought was your biggest flaw? For most people, it's never! They don't ask, because they don't really want to know the answer! If we were more open to receiving constructive feedback, perhaps we could make an intelligent assessment about our strengths and weaknesses and make the appropriate changes to help ourselves.

The next time I saw Sally, she was still a little confused about what had happened at the firm, and it was clear that no one had taken the time to speak with her about the perception that the state of her office had created within the firm. The one thing that is often not taken into consideration is that some behaviors that are acceptable in our homes, or the homes in which we were raised, are not acceptable in the workplace. Unfortunately, some people have to learn the hard way.

It takes courage to receive criticism from others; however, when it is constructive, it is very effective as a tool for growth. It's one thing to have a mentor to help us with our decisions and paths, but it's another thing to have the people closest to you make a personal assessment of your personality, behavior, and other traits. Yes, you are vulnerable to a certain extent, but if you wish to grow and develop, there can be power in vulnerability.

FRIENDS AND FEEDBACK EXERCISE

This exercise takes some courage, but you may be surprised and enlightened by the results. Write down a list of five individuals know you well who preferably live in your city.

1. _____

2. _____

3. _____

4. _____

5. _____

Either call or e-mail each of these individuals and tell them that you are reading a book about success and are working on your own personal self-development and growth. Share with them that part of this book focuses on shortcomings and aspects of your personality, disposition, behavioral traits, and essentially how you are perceived by others. Get these five people together in one space and ask them to answer the following ten questions, with honesty. You can give them the list of questions on a separate piece of paper and ask them to type the answers so that you won't know who has written what. Meet again after seven days or so and allow everyone to have a chance to put their survey in the same envelope to keep it anonymous. It's important for the individual filling out the questionnaire to know that it is anonymous so that they are completely honest with their feedback. Let them know that there will be no further questions asked (unless they wish to discuss it further) and that there will be no retribution for their honesty, opinions, and thoughts.

"Once we know our weaknesses, they cease to do us harm."
                                        - Unknown

The idea here is to uncover facets of your personality and traits that could be hindering your success. You will want to explore these areas to gain new insight and opportunities (and use others to serve as motivators).

Questions
1. What do you like most about me?
2. What do I excel at (what are my strengths)?
3. What are my weaknesses?
4. What would be the one thing you would change about me?
5. What is my biggest excuse?
6. If there were three things that you think I could do right now to make my life better (whether it is in the area of my relationships, finances, health, career, or spirituality), what would it be?
7. Is there anything that you've always wanted to tell me but haven't?
8. What five words would you use to describe me to someone who doesn't know me (both positive and negative)?
9. What strength do you think I could capitalize on?
10. What other feedback can you provide for me to help me with my growth/development?

When you receive the answers to these questions, use them as tools for growth. Look for recurring themes, areas that you'd never thought about in terms of improvement, and other people's perceptions about you in terms of your strengths. Use this information to gain clarity in areas that you didn't think needed work but, if you did work on them, could take you further in your growth and development. Remember, this exercise is for you, not an opportunity to start probing and interrogating those who filled out the survey. Honest opinions can sometimes be painful to hear, but the beauty of them is that sometimes it's exactly what we need to hear to help us get to the next level of success.

"Don't mind criticism. If it is untrue, disregard it. If it is unfair, keep from irritation; if it is ignorant, smile. If it is justified it is not criticism, learn from it."
                                          - Unknown

Journals

"I don't want to live in a hand-me-down world of others' experiences. I want to write about me, my discoveries, my fears, my feelings, about me."
                                    - Helen Keller

I have been writing journals since I was 14. I actually can't remember what prompted me to do so. I believe that I just had so many thoughts, ideas, and emotions that I had to get them out of my head and onto paper. Now, more than 20 years later, I have boxes and boxes of journals. It may be every day, every week, or once a month that I will write an entry about how I'm feeling, my thoughts about the world around me, the people in my life, my goals, etc. I write it all down. For me, writing in a journal does three things. First, it is a very cathartic and peaceful exercise. Most of the time, I'll curl up on the sofa in a space where there are no distractions and write. Sometimes it's a couple of sentences; sometimes it's endless pages. When I am stressed, writing in my journal is a wonderful stress reliever, and I feel so much better after I have communicated with the pages and fleshed out my thoughts. For me, putting my thoughts on paper acts as a source of clarity.

Second, writing is a tool for growth. When I go back ten years, or five years, or even last month, I can see how much I've grown in certain areas of my life, and how little in others. I can see behavioral traits that didn't serve me when I was in my early twenties, but I find myself doing those same things today. It serves as a powerful reminder that helps to shift behavior. My journal acts as a reminder of what not to do, what not to repeat, the types of people to surround myself with, or emotions that I need to work through because of the effects they had on me ten years ago. I am reminded of certain things that I liked to do, thoughts and feelings that I felt back then, and ways in which I was able to deal with issues. It shows me what may be able to help me now and helps me flesh out ideas, dreams, and aspirations as well as doubts, fears, and frustrations. We can learn so much more about ourselves by communicating with ourselves and then reviewing that communication.

Third, a journal provides me with a space to dream, discover, and expand. I write about my future desires, what I hope to accomplish in the years ahead, and where I want to be at certain points of my life. It's great to see what I wanted for myself at ages 25, 30, and 35 and whether or not I achieved those things. It is also a great confidence booster when you can read about some of the things you wanted and then look at the reality of the situation to see that you were right on point. When you are able to articulate and put those things down on paper, you are taking the first step in making those dreams a reality. You start to develop ideas about those dreams, and then you start to move toward those goals quickly.

"Keep a grateful journal. Every night list five things that you are grateful for. What it will begin to do is change your perspective of your day and your life."
— Oprah Winfrey

Purchase a journal from your local bookstore and start recording your thoughts today. Keep it by your bedside (providing you have trusted people around you who won't read it) or in a safe place. It's okay if you aren't able to write every day, just make sure that you write in it at least once a week. My advice would be to start off with an entry once a week, and then just go from there. Our thoughts and feelings change so rapidly from day to day and hour to hour, you will soon want to be able to catch your thoughts and feelings frequently. As you begin to write, you will begin to learn so much more about yourself, and as you learn more about yourself you will be able to use the information as a rich source of knowledge.

"I haven't written for a few days, because I wanted first of all to think about my diary. It's an odd idea for someone like me to keep a diary; not only because I have never done so before, but because it seems to me that neither I—nor for that matter anyone else—will be interested in the unbosomings of a thirteen-year-old school girl. Still, what does that matter? I want to write, but more than that, I want to bring out all kinds of things that lie buried deep in my heart."

— Anne Frank: The Diary of a Young Girl [1952]

chapter 8

The Reputation Ripple

I have named this chapter "The Reputation Ripple" because of the ripple effect a good or bad reputation can have on you. Your reputation is essentially what other people believe to be true about you—your habits, work ethic, personality, character, skills, etc. It is something that is built over time. You've all heard the phrase "Your reputation precedes you." Well, that couldn't be more true. People are offered jobs based on their reputations; they are given promotions and introduced to other people based on their reputations. Many build wealth based solely on their reputations, and the doors of opportunity are continually opened because of reputations. Having said all that, your reputation is a very fragile thing. While it can take years to build and maintain a positive reputation, it can also be destroyed in minutes. One key to career success is to build a great reputation and have the ripple effect work for you in a positive way.

> "It seems that we learn lessons when we least expect them but always when we need them most, and the true "gift" in these lessons always lies in the learning process itself."
> - Cathy Lee Crosby

We know that reputation is important, but how do you build one? What do you want to be known for? Do you want to be known as someone that is on time for everything, as a sharp dresser, as someone who gets things done, as someone who is honest, smart, and reliable? Hopefully, you want to be known for all of the above. If that is the case, then your reputation is built by continually exhibiting these positive traits. You don't just follow through on projects once or twice; you follow through on them all the time. You aren't just on time for work one day out of the week; you're on time all the time. You don't just contribute to the success of a company sometimes; you do it all the time. It's about being consistent. Your actions are everything. Are you a person that sticks to your word? If your management team asks you to submit a report next week on Tuesday at noon, do they know that you are one of those individuals that will submit it on Tuesday at noon, or will they expect you to submit it late (because you're known for being unreliable)? If you completed the exercise in Chapter 7, "Knowledge Is Power," you may be able to get some insight into what your reputation is like presently.

I have a couple of stories about the reputation ripple that highlight the importance of having a good reputation.

Many years ago, when I was managing a team of sales executives, there was one account executive in particular that was very talented, let's call her Jane. Jane was smart, dressed well, and was great with the clients. In fact, I would often give her many of the most important clients because I knew that she would take good care of them. I would always hear great things about the networking events that she attended and tales of the business that was going to be forthcoming because of the great conversations Jane had had with prospects. One week after I returned to work from a vacation, I heard about the success of one of the biggest networking events in the city. I asked Jane to write a list of all the individuals she had met and what her thoughts were about the possibility of developing business with them. I received an impressive report with some great names and some good insight into how we might strategically develop business with their companies. That week, as normal, I submitted my expense reports for the team, which included the $300 that Jane had expended on the fee to attend the event. A few weeks later, I received a call from one of the vice presidents of the company, questioning the $300 entry fee for the event. The VP in question was close friends with Jane, and it turned out that on that particular evening they had been at another party and not at the networking event Jane had reported attending. When I asked Jane directly whether she had gone to the event or not, she admitted that she had lied about her attendance at the event. Jane's reputation crumbled in a matter of minutes, not only with me, but also with the whole management team and others who eventually heard about what happened. All the great work that Jane had done up until that time became a distant memory, and she was seen as a thief, a liar, and an untrustworthy person. Questions were immediately raised about all the other events that she had attended as well as about her employment with the company. Everything she did from that point forward was subject to scrutiny. Were her self-proclaimed successes to date fabricated? Were any of the reports on business development meetings she said she had attended true? Her whole career with the company was questioned. Of course, it didn't take long before she left the company, because her reputation was in tatters and there was little she could do to bounce back.

The story doesn't end there, however (this is where the ripple comes into effect). A few years later, I received a call from a senior executive at another company who asked me about Jane. They were thinking about offering her a position within their company, and wanted me to tell them about Jane's reliability and trustworthiness. Of course, I couldn't answer in a positive manner, because of the information that I had. If I had answered in the affirmative, I would have been compromising my integrity, which could in turn have affected my reputation. Ultimately, the company didn't approach her because of my candid feedback.

Now, let's take that ripple effect one step further. The executive who called me to find out about Jane has a network too, and if Jane's name came up again, what do you think would have happened? The ripple effect can work very quickly, and before you know it, people know you for a set of behavioral traits that they believe to be true. Don't underestimate how small industries are, from city to city, state to state, and country to country. People in the same industry tend to cluster together and move in the same circles. Also, with the advent of globalization and social networking, it's easy to contact and connect with people who know who you are and what kind of reputation you have.

> "Don't consider your reputation and you may do anything you like."   **- Chinese proverb**

On the other end of the spectrum, let me tell you a story about another one of my former associates, Patricia. Patricia was an executive at one of the large media companies in Atlanta. She had climbed the corporate ladder moving from one promotion to the next, because everyone knew her as someone who got things done, she was a leader and was very effective in her execution of any project. She also had a great ability to bring teams together and get them to work efficiently. Her communication skills were considered to be top-notch, and she was quoted often for her expertise in industry periodicals. Many years after Patricia had been working for the media company, she decided to take a year off to start a family. After the year was over, she started to seek out positions and called a few individuals she knew who

84

were still in the industry. No less than a week later, she had received over six calls from companies that wanted to bring her on board. Offers ranged from companies in New York City to Los Angeles, from VP-level positions to equity share offers. It was really quite impressive. What do you think caused those offers to come in so quickly? After all, Patricia had been out of the industry and off the market for well over a year. Clearly, it was the reputation she held before she left. Reputations can last a very, very long time, and sometimes it's all you have to go on. The industry had changed somewhat by the time she was ready to return, but it didn't matter, because Patricia had the qualities that people valued. As a result, they wanted her to be a part of their organizations. The great thing was that Patricia didn't even have to put a resume together to get another position; the offers that came forth were based solely on her *reputation*.

> "In life, your reputation is the only thing that can take you to the top of the mountain or the bottom of a gutter in a matter of minutes…"
> **- Erica Moore-Burton**

References

Any time you apply for a job, your prospective employer will ask for your references. Who do you have that can vouch for your work ethic, your work product, and your reputation? Prospective employers want to know that you are who you say you are or purport to be. It's one thing to sit in front of a prospective employer and espouse all the good qualities you believe that you have; it's another thing when they can call someone you have worked with in the past who can say the same things. As an executive recruiter, I always found it a bit odd and suspicious when someone gave me references that were five to ten years old. Unless you have been out of the work force, or you have a compelling reason why you can't produce more recent references, this is definitely a red flag. If you can't get anyone from the company where you most recently worked to vouch for you, that is a sign that there may have been some issues. I know many companies that have policies that prohibit them from giving professional references, because of liability issues; however, there usually is someone with whom you've built a relationship who can vouch for you. Make sure you always have recent references on hand that will serve you well as you make your way up the career ladder.

Also, when you are giving references for other people, never underestimate what vouching for someone else is doing for your reputation. If you espouse qualities about a person that are eventually proven to be untrue, your trustworthiness, integrity, and judgment will most certainly be called into question.

Excellence In Small Things

You can start to build or further build your reputation by being a person of your word and choosing excellence in everything you do. Start with excellence in small things, and it will lead to excellence in the larger things in your life. Be known as a person of your word; when you say you're going to do something, make sure that you do it. Make your word count for something. As you begin to master excellence, your reputation will start to improve all aspects of your life. As we have said, building your reputation takes time, practice, and consistency. Just because you were reliable once doesn't mean that you're going to be reliable again. You have to be reliable 5, 10, or 15 times in order to be known as someone who is reliable.

REPUTATION RIPPLE EXERCISE

1. List ten things for which you want to be known.
2. Describe the kind of reputation you have (include both positive and negative things).
3. List areas of your reputation you need to work on.
4. List steps you can take today to start restoring the parts of your reputation that need work and to build those that you want to be known for (list five things)?

Start building your reputation today. It will serve you in many great ways in the years ahead. Once you have built a good reputation in one area, protect it fiercely. There will be times on your journey when you will need to rely on it heavily because it is all you may have.

"Your reputation is built on the things you do consistently."
— Erica Moore-Burton

chapter 9

Health and Success

Do you have the energy for success? Take a look at the people you deem to be successful and take note of their energy levels. Do they seem energetic to you? Are they constantly getting things done? Do they live healthy lifestyles? Your health is one of the most important things you can take care of. Without good health, life can be very difficult and present challenges that prevent you from reaching your goals and life long dreams. When we talk about maintaining good health, this includes having a healthy diet, a regular fitness program, and a healthy state of mind.

Fitness

Staying fit should be the number one priority in our lives. When you are able to stay fit and healthy, you can take advantage of everything that life has to offer. However, for many, maintaining a healthy lifestyle can be very difficult. It's much easier to sit in front of the television watching your favorite show than it is to go out and get some exercise. For those who have a difficult time maintaining a healthy level of fitness, the key is to think about your goals and dreams. Having a reason for living can act as a motivating force to help you stay fit and make sure that your health is a top priority. So, when you think about health and fitness, you are not only keeping fit for the sake of keeping fit, but also as a motivating force behind the action. If you keep your goals and dreams at the forefront of your mind, it can help you continue to maintain a healthy lifestyle. Whether it's a matter of being healthy so you can continue to climb the corporate ladder, maintain your hobbies, or to be fit for your children, spouse or aging parents—use your goals to help you. Health and success go hand in hand.

If you can't commit to exercising every day, commit to three times a week and increase the amount a little each month. If scheduling time to exercise is difficult, find certain times of the day that will work for you. Get creative. Are you able to go for a power walk during your lunch hour or for a 15-minute walk during an afternoon break? Can you get into the habit of waking up 40 minutes earlier to exercise before your day gets started? Getting into the habit of exercising in the morning can be challenging at first. But, once you are able to do it consistently, exercising is the best feeling in the world, and you will feel a great sense of accomplishment.

Maintaining a good level of fitness can help you reduce stress levels and cope with the demands of your business and personal life. It can also help you increase your energy levels dramatically. Watch how healthy people move and notice their disposition and mood levels. If you have the energy to do more in life, the possibilities are boundless. I have known many people throughout my career who have kept unhealthy lifestyles by not exercising at all or maintaining very bad eating habits. Some of those individuals have had to take time off work to deal with health issues, and some have been unable to keep up with the demands of their careers. These things essentially caused them to fall behind on the pay scale as well as miss out on promotions and other personal and professional opportunities.

> "He who has health has hope. He who has hope has everything."
> - Proverb

As mentioned, the benefits of exercise can be amazing. Did you know that exercise could improve your mood and general disposition? Exercising can help you deal with the demands of life in general. Whenever I am feeling a little low for one reason or another, I head to my kickboxing class. Once I'm in there kicking and punching to the sounds of Beyonce, Shakira, and Seal, my mood levels are lifted immediately, and I am put in a much better state of mind. As you exercise, a substance called endorphins are released by the brain. When these endorphins are released, they produce feelings of euphoria and general well-being and naturally boost your mood. Imagine the effect that feeling good about life most of the time can have on your level of success!

"Every human being is the author of his own health or disease."
                                                    - Buddha

If you have difficulty maintaining an exercise routine, enlist a friend to work out with you. Having a friend who you work out with makes you accountable to someone. I often arrange to meet a friend at 5:30 in the morning at my local track. I haven't missed one session with her - why? Because when I know that someone is relying on me to be there, I'm not going to let that person down. Remember we talked about reputation and accountability in the previous chapter. When someone else is counting on me to be there, I'm going to be there, because I don't want to be known as unreliable and untrustworthy. I want to be a person of my word, so I show up without fail. This can really help you get your exercise routine started. Join a gym with a friend and make a commitment to each other to be there on a certain day every week. If you don't have any friends you can do this with, perhaps enlist the help of a fitness coach. When you are paying someone to help you that can also increase your sense of accountability. Moreover, you are unlikely to want to waste your money. A fitness coach will certainly keep you accountable, because you are paying him or her to help you maintain a fitness plan that works for you.

If you don't enjoy going to the gym or traditional exercise classes, instead of meeting a friend for coffee go for a long walk together. Try a dance class or a sport, perhaps tennis, racquetball, rollerblading, or cycling. Try something that you've never done before! Try out many different things until you find something that fits with your temperament, personality, and fitness level. As your fitness level increases, challenge yourself and change your routine. I like to change my routine every few months for a couple of reasons: I can exercise different sets of muscles, and I can try something new so that I don't get bored easily. Sign up for charitable events such as 5K walks, or even challenge yourself to a marathon. It's a fun way to get in shape and a great way to meet new people.

Healthy Diets

A healthy diet goes hand in hand with exercise. It doesn't matter if you have a great exercise regime; if you eat poorly, it really defeats the whole purpose. Healthy eating means that you have a diet filled with fresh fruit and vegetables and that you drink plenty of water. Again, if you need assistance in this area of your life, engage the services of a nutritionist or find an accountability partner. There are so many fad diets on the market and, if the truth were told, none of them really work. What does work is simply maintaining a regular exercise regime and eating a well-balanced and healthy diet. It's really as simple as that. When you have both under control, and you feel good about the way you look, how your clothes feel and fit, and your energy levels are high, you will have the ability to focus on more things in your life. Obviously, the opposite is also true: when you are carrying extra weight around and are always struggling with your wardrobe, it can have a detrimental effect on your overall sense of well-being and self-esteem. I know that it is easier said than done: this is one area of my life that I have had the most challenges with over the years. If you're anything like me and have a sweet tooth, it can get you into lots of trouble. What I have done in this area of my life is to use accountability partners, enroll in exercise programs to help with the accountability piece, and use alternative foods (dried fruits) to help curb my craving for sweets. Water isn't my favorite beverage, so to help maintain my intake of eight glasses a day, I add lime to it. This adds a bit of sizzle to the taste. Get creative with your diet and exercise. It will help you in the long run if you do.

Health and Fitness
EXERCISE:

1. I want to be healthy for:

a._____

b._____

c._____

d._____

e._____

2. If I had more energy, I could accomplish:

a._____

b._____

c._____

d._____

e._____

3. I will commit to exercising at least ____ times per week.

4. I will try one of the following activities within the next four weeks (e.g., tennis, walking, horse-riding, rollerblading, dancing):

a._____

b._____

c._____

d._____

e._____

5. List five creative ways that you can stay on track and implement them today!

a._____

b._____

c._____

d._____

e._____

chapter 10

No Limits!

Imagine if you could live a life of no limits. What would your life look like? Where would you live? What would you do on a daily basis? Who would you surround yourself with? Where would you travel? How does that feel: great, fantastic, perhaps intimidating, or a little of each? Living a life of no limits is something that anyone can achieve, but it does take courage and confidence.

> "You can have anything you want if you want it desperately enough. You must want it with an inner exuberance that erupts through the skin and joins the energy that created the world."
>
> – **Sheila Graham**

I haven't always lived a life of no limits, but in the moments that I have, life has tasted so much sweeter. Living a life with no limits means really going for it, getting things done regardless of the obstacles, facing challenges head on, not worrying about things you can't control, taking responsibility, living fearlessly, tasting life, experiencing the colors, smells and feelings of life, appreciating nature, being open and non-judgmental, being vulnerable at times, not being afraid to laugh at yourself, hugging life with both arms and squeezing it tight, treating it as though it was the most precious gift that anyone could have given you!

Before we get into the details of this chapter, I want you to read the above paragraph again, and then write in the space on the next page:

In order to start living a life of no limits today, I will:

_____
_____
_____
_____
_____
_____
_____
_____
_____
_____

Taking Responsibility

Taking responsibility is the first step to living a successful life of no limits. It's about taking responsibility for yourself, your journey, and your actions. I have always found it strange when I have met people who are struggling with certain parts of their lives, but don't take responsibility for it. When I probe a bit, I often discover that these people always have an excuse for the state of their affairs. They blame their parents, friends, co-workers, acquaintances … even their pets! You know what happens when you point your finger at someone else, right? Well, try it. Point your finger out right now at all those people that are at fault in your life. Look at your hand carefully. Did you notice that there are three fingers pointing back at you? "ME," I hear you say, "ME" you scream in awe. How can it possibly be "ME? It's THEM!!!" Try it any way you want to. Try your left hand just to be sure. Yes, surprise! There are still three fingers pointing back at you!

"I have always regarded myself as the pillar of my life."
                                                   - Meryl Streep

The point here is that in order to live a successful life, you have to take responsibility for yourself. This means taking responsibility for your actions, your attitudes, your faults, your mistakes, and everything! I am always surprised when I meet someone who is blaming something or someone else from ten years ago for the things that are going wrong today. Living in a negative past doesn't help you gain a positive future, you are the only person who can take responsibility for your present and appreciate it for the gift that it is. In these types of scenarios, the people who are being blamed have moved on and are living their lives. Meanwhile the self-appointed victim is holding onto issues that are preventing him or her from growing and living life to the fullest. We may not be able to control what happens to us or what people do to us; but, we have choices and the ability to choose our responses to these situations.

My philosophy is that you have to stop blaming and start doing. Do whatever it takes to help move you forward and continue to grow. To live a life of no limits means that you continually are taking responsibility for your own well-being, happiness, attitude, choices, and even repercussions. If you haven't read the book written by my husband, Chappale Linn Burton, entitled "How To Choose Happiness... Most of The Time," I highly recommend that you do, and not just because he is my husband! He has a remarkable story that is so inspiring it has helped many people change their perspective about life. His story is one of triumph over tragedy. While he could have blamed so many people for his tragic past, he used the challenges he faced to fuel a passion-filled life with no limits. I like to look at life as a canvas, on which you can choose what pictures to draw and what colors to use. You get to choose whether you create a crazy, zany, vibrant masterpiece or a striking, rich and extravagant collage. You get to choose, so why waste time and expend energy blaming others? You get to choose everything right here and right now.

"In the long run we shape our lives, and we shape ourselves. The process never ends until we die. And the choices we make are ultimately our own responsibility."

— Eleanor Roosevelt

Shake It Up - Get Uncomfortable
Feel the Fear and Go Forth!

Living a life of no limits means that you have to shake things up sometimes and have the courage to be uncomfortable. Every time I have gotten a promotion over the years, I have felt a little uncomfortable about the role at first, but it has been a good feeling of discomfort. Why? Because when I'm uncomfortable, I know it means I am about to grow in some way. Ultimately, I want to be comfortable again, but I know there is a bridge that I will have to cross, something I am going to have to learn, or a challenge I need to undertake. In order to grow and get comfortable with the new level, I have to step it up! By stepping it up, I am inevitably growing, because I am learning everything that I need to know to get that level of comfort again. In the process, I am taking another step on the rung of my success ladder. Being uncomfortable can be a scary experience, but like anything, once you dive in, you often find that it's not that bad after all.

"Let women be provided with living strength of their own."

— Simone DeBeauvoir

When I talk about discomfort at my workshops, I always retell the story of when I first came to America over ten years ago. It was one of the most uncomfortable experiences I ever had. I was moving to a new country where I didn't have any friends, family, or job and only $800 in my pocket to start a new life. (It's not like going to college where you have a structure in place and can almost instantly start meeting people in your dorms.) I had decided to move from England to Atlanta back in the 1990s. I was very comfortable in England—I had my parents, siblings, friends, and a good job. Life was moving along nicely, and I was very secure. However, what I yearned for was growth of some sort, and taking a class just wasn't going to be enough for me. After several months of thinking about it, I decided one afternoon that I was going to take a leap and move to America.

I can distinctly remember what I did next. I took out an atlas in my parent's living room and scanned the map of America, from east to west, north to south. One of the things that I always disliked about England was the weather, so that really was on the top of my list in terms of criteria for my new home. I always had it in my mind that Florida was a place for retirees (I didn't know too much about South Beach back then!). New York was appealing, but I had been there many times and thought that in some ways it was very similar to London. That wouldn't do, because I wanted to be uncomfortable! I thought about Los Angeles (where I reside now), but it was a little too far away. I ended up choosing Atlanta, Georgia. Of course, I had the naysayers around me. I heard all the reasons why I should not go to America; especially the South! The list was long and ranged from the violence that we saw on television to the fact that I didn't have a job, I didn't know anybody, and had only $800 to my name. Well, that all may have been true, but I also created a list of all of my strengths at the time, and it included the fact that I had an education, a knack for meeting people and making friends, ambition, confidence, and the most important ingredient, faith. A month later, I was saying goodbye to my friends and family at the airport. It was one of the hardest things that I have ever had to do, but it also was the most exhilarating, because I knew that I was about to embark upon an exciting adventure in the United States.

Did I feel a little uncomfortable? Well, that is an understatement! The one thing I knew for sure was that I was going to become a different person with all the inevitable personal growth that was about to take place. In order to pursue my goals, I had to adjust not only to this new country, but also to a southern state and a completely different culture. When the naysayers would discuss the things I didn't have, I would always retort that I could always "return to base," meaning I could always go back to where I started.

> "I plunged into the job of creating something from nothing ... though I hadn't a penny left, I considered cash money as the smallest part of my resources. I had faith in a living god, faith in myself, and a desire to serve."
>
> **- Mary McLeod Bethune**

Whether it's an exam that you're nervous about taking, a new role that you've taken on, a new business that you're starting, or a new career altogether—ask yourself, "What is the worst that can happen?" Make a list of all those things, and then ask yourself, "If the worst did happen, would it really be earth-shattering?" The answer will vary from situation to situation. But, if the worst that could happen will not harm your health, your family and friends will still love you, and you will still have the capacity to appreciate life, how bad could it really be? Sometimes, the thing we fear most is our own success. Many people look for excuses not to be successful. It goes back to that blame game that we talked about earlier and not taking responsibility for our own thoughts and actions.

"How very little can be done under the spirit of fear."   **- Florence Nightingale**

I challenge you today, right now, to do something that you're not necessarily comfortable with and create a corresponding list of the absolute worst things that could happen if you started on a journey to accomplish your goals.

Earlier I shared with you a technique that I used to pass the bar exam. But, even before getting to that point, there were some challenges. I received my legal education in London, England, so many years ago when I decided to take the bar exam here in the United States, I was very nervous. Well, it didn't take long before the naysayers appeared. The first one was a lawyer I knew. She lectured me extensively over coffee about the fact that I hadn't received my legal education in this country; therefore, it was going to be impossible for me to pass the exam. She literally went down a list of all the reasons I wasn't going to pass, including the fact that I had chosen one of the hardest bars in the country to take! Another attorney I worked with at the time remarked that my effort to take the bar was "rather ambitious." Well, it turns out that they were right. I studied for the bar and failed in my first attempt. For a few months afterward, I wallowed in self-pity and felt a little silly for trying to take one of the hardest bar exams in the country. It was around that time that I really started working on myself and my mindset. After some introspection, I decided one afternoon that I would examine my fears. It was then that I came across this excerpt by Marianne Williamson:

Our Deepest Fear

"Our worst fear is not that we are inadequate.
Our deepest fear is that we are powerful beyond
measure.
It is our light not our darkness that most frightens us.
We ask ourselves,
Who am I not to be brilliant, gorgeous, talented,
fabulous?
Actually, who are you not to be?
You are a child of God.
Your playing small does not serve the world.
There is nothing enlightening about shrinking
so that other
People won't feel insecure around you.
We are meant to shine, as children do.
We were born to make manifest the glory of God within
It is not just in some of us; it is in everyone
And as we let our own light shine, we unconsciously
Give other people the permission to do the same"
- Marianne Williamson

After reading this quote, I made a list of the worst things that could happen if I failed again. My list looked a little something like this:

- I would be embarrassed to fail a second time.
- I would have to stay an assistant for the rest of my life.
- I would spend three months of my life studying again without a successful result.
- I would waste thousands of dollars.
- I couldn't be a lawyer and would never find any other profession that I would be fulfilled with.
- Failing is not fun.

The list went on and on. I started to examine how bad some of these things REALLY were and whether they were based on "FEAR," which actually stands for False Evidence Appearing Real. So what if I didn't pass a second time; at least I had the courage to try. Would I really have to be an assistant for the rest of my life? Were there really no other professions in the world? Surely, I would be smarter after three months of studying the same materials. I'm sure that I could spend thousands of dollars on something more frivolous, like clothes and makeup, without gaining the courage, strength, and knowledge that was necessary to get through it again. So, whatever the result, it was money well invested. Once I examined what I really feared and discovered there was nothing to be afraid of, I threw my list in the trash and set about studying again for my second attempt. I enlisted the mechanisms that I talked about earlier, such as goal setting, visualization, and taking action. Then I ignored the naysayers and focused on studying (and studying only) for three months. As you know, the second time around, things were much different; I passed the New York State Bar Exam. My point here is to ask yourself questions that will help you uncover the root of your fear; then, feel the fear and go forth!

"If you let fear of consequence prevent you from following your deepest instinct, then your life will be safe, expedient and thin."

- Katharine Butler Hathaway

FEEL THE FEAR AND GO FORTH! EXERCISE

1. Describe a goal that you would like to accomplish, but would fear doing.
2. List the benefits of reaching this goal.
3. What is the worst that could happen? (List as many consequences as you can.)
4. How bad would these things be on a scale of one to ten? (Consider questions like the ones below):
   a) Would you have supporters, whether they are members of your family or friends?
   b) Would you still be alive?
   c) Would you still have your health?
   d) Would you be enhancing your life or other people's lives by fulfilling and accomplishing this goal?
   e) Would you be making a valuable contribution to the world?
5. Will you grow as a result of reaching this goal? For example, will you be wiser, gain a new skill, or practice resilience or courage that could be used in another area of your life, or learn how to do something new?

Take the time to do this exercise, and really challenge yourself to think about the answers. Once you have examined them and discovered that your fear is false evidence appearing real – which it is most of the time, go forth courageously and head toward your goal with zest! Changing your perspective and being comfortable with being uncomfortable can be one of the most powerful things you can do for your growth and development.

"I have found adventure in flying, in world travel, in business, and even close at hand... adventure is a state of mind – and spirit. It comes with faith, for with complete faith, there is no fear of what faces you in life or death."
                                        - Jacqueline Cochran

chapter 11

Service

> "Service is the rent we pay for the privilege of living on this earth."
> — **Shirley Chisholm**

How many people do you serve on a daily basis? From the moment you wake up to the moment you sleep, how many people do you serve? Service is the foundation of success; the more people you serve, and add value to their lives, the higher the likelihood of your success. It is really as simple as that. The laws of the universe are real, and just as we talked about success attracting success earlier, the same is true of service. If service is the foundation of success, it has to be true that success is a direct result. I am of the opinion that we are all here on earth to share whatever gift God has given to us. Each of us has at least one gift. For some it is recognized from the moment they start walking. For others, it takes years to discover it, or years to start sharing it with the world. When you serve others, you too will be served, whether it's in the form of happiness, love, peace of mind, or even money.

Success Attracts Success
Service is the Foundation of Success

Think of the most giving person you know: a person who is giving of herself, her time, resources, money, or love. Has that person achieved any level of success? Whether success is measured in terms of her level of happiness, the abundance of love in her life, monetary success, the time people are willing to spend with her, or the lengths to which people are willing to go to do things for her, the answer is probably yes.

> "What I know for sure is that what you give comes back to you."
> — Oprah Winfrey

When some people think of service, they think of things like time, and money. There are many ways in which you can serve others that can help you lead a successful life. As you give of yourself, the world will give back to you.

> "Purposeful giving is not as apt to deplete one's resources; it belongs to that natural order of giving that seems to renew itself even in the act of depletion."
> — Anne Morrow Lindbergh

Serving Those Around You

Many years ago, I had a manager called Sam. Sam was smart and had a seemingly successful business. I worked as an assistant for him, along with three other assistants. We would barely even get a "good morning" when he walked into the office. In fact, I would often arrive to work in the morning only to find another assistant in tears because of something unpleasant he had said or done.

Sam drove a nice car and had all the accoutrements of success, but I noticed him many times just sitting and staring out of the window looking desperately unhappy. Sam was single, and he didn't seem to treat any woman he was dating very well either. It always seemed as though his date needed to fit into his "successful" life. As a result, he was never lucky in love. He would micromanage his staff, and one day he even said to one of the other assistants, "It's so great to be rich isn't it? Oh, I'm sorry, you wouldn't know about that, would you?" I was appalled, especially since I knew that the assistant was a single mother struggling to support her daughter. Time went on, and bit by bit his business started to deteriorate and mistakes started to be made on important projects. At one point, things got very busy at the office but none of the support staff were willing to come in on the weekends to help or put forward any more energy than necessary. On a daily basis, he was serving people for financial gain, but he was miserable; he had a staff that didn't respect him, and his business certainly wasn't thriving as much as it could have been. What would this picture look like if Sam had "served" his staff on a daily basis with a smile and "good morning," treated people with respect for the work they were doing for his business, and served their natural talents? I have seen CEOs and managers over the years "serve" their staff and the results in many cases have been remarkable. The relationships resulted in high productivity and commitment levels that made the employees want to do whatever it took to make the business successful. As the businesses thrived, so have the owners, and much of it has been attributed to their attitude towards their staff. Ego did not play a big role.

> "Sow good services, sweet remembrances will grow them."
> — **Madame de Stael**

You can start to serve today. You can do something as simple as smile at people! By smiling you are doing two things: you are giving a kind expression to others and increasing your own feelings of well-being. You can serve by helping a co-worker with a project, by buying coffee for your whole team, by volunteering to teach a class at a halfway house, or by visiting someone in a retirement home. In a single day, there are hundreds of ways you can serve. Can you give up your seat on the train for someone else? Can you let someone else in while driving? How about holding an elevator door open for someone else? By consciously serving others, your good deeds will come back to you and your life will be enhanced greatly. If you want to serve in a larger capacity, think about whether you can contribute to a large event that is happening in your city or distributing food at a local food bank. Perhaps even think about starting your own online blog. It is up to you to choose how many people you serve, just remember, the more you serve, the better.

I have often found that there is much disdain for the large amounts of money paid to celebrities, basketball players, and other artists. Many people don't think they are deserving of the large checks they receive for their work. Well, I am of the opinion that these people deserve every single cent they earn. Why? Well, just look at the number of people they serve. They serve millions and millions of people by sharing their art and skill. For that, they are deserving. At the same time, many people will argue that people like teachers deserve more money because they serve our children. Although I think this is true, I will say that most of the teachers I know are very fulfilled by their profession. The difference that they are making in the lives of the children gives them a huge sense of gratification. (Remember, success doesn't just mean making money.) I also know of teachers who feel that success is making a lot of money as well as making a difference in people's lives. They have opted for a different kind of teaching—the kind of teaching that reaches millions of people around the world—and as a direct result, they are making a lot of money. Oprah Winfrey, Suzie Orman, and Lisa Nichols are great examples.

Giving Back

On a month-to-month basis, examine whether you are giving of your time or your money. Volunteering can be an amazing experience on so many levels. As we said before, as you give of yourself, the world gives back to you in so many ways. There are so many worthy organizations and community initiatives that need volunteers, whether it is for a one-time occasion or an ongoing opportunity. Whether you have one hour a month or one hour a week, give back to your community and make it a personal goal to, in some way, leave the world a little better than when you arrived.

At a time when people are concerned about their finances and their jobs, this is, in fact, the best time to give. The concept of energy flow is in place when we give money, and as you freely give of your time and money, money will flow back to you. When you hold on to it tightly and are afraid to give it away because you believe you won't have enough for yourself, you essentially stop the flow to you.

"If my hands are fully occupied in holding on to something, I can neither give nor receive."
                                                          - Dorothy Solle

SERVICE EXERCISE

1. List the ways in which you have served in the last six months.
2. List five ways in which you can serve in the next six months.
3. Take action this week on one of the ways in which you can serve.
4. List three charities that you will commit to supporting (whether in time or money) in the next six months.
5. Visit www.VolunteerMatch.org and research ways in which you can volunteer in your community today!

chapter 12

Placing Your Order

"Be of good cheer. Do not think of today's failures but of the success that may come tomorrow. You have set yourselves a difficult task, but
you will succeed if you persevere; and you will
find a joy in overcoming obstacles. Remember,
no effort that we make to attain something
beautiful is ever lost."

- Helen Keller

Success Comes To Those Who Ask For It

I have long said that children are the best sales people in the
world. Have you noticed what children do when they want
something from their parents? They ask for it, then ask for it
again, then ask for it again, and again, and again. Many may
see this behavior as being a pest. I, on the other hand, look
at it as being persistent, and in life persistence is what you
need to be successful. Sometimes the world doesn't give you
what you ask the first time around, so you have to ask again,
again, and again. It's not that the world doesn't want to give
you what you want. It may simply be that there is a journey
upon which you must embark in order to learn or become
prepared to receive that gift or perhaps another one.

We have gone through many techniques and principles that
can help you on your journey. You may have heard the phrase
that 'It is about the journey and who we become during that
journey, and not the destination'. Well, this is so very true.
One thing that is a common factor among most successful
people is that success is a way of life for them. They are
continually working on being successful, from even their

smallest actions. Their biggest successes are the results of many smaller victories.

Whatever you want in this world can be yours; the sky is really the limit. Ask the world for what you want by declaring it in written form. Tell friends, associates, and others in your network about it. Then, start your plan of action. An important thing to remember is to ensure that you are prepared and ready to receive exactly what you request. When you ask for something and start your personal journey toward it, the opportunity can arise at anytime; so, you want to be in a place where you are prepared and ready to take advantage.

The world is getting smaller, and with the advent of the Internet and all the amazing resources around us, you can have anything that you declare you want.

I hope you will take some crucial steps by completing all the exercises in this book. Take one step at a time and move toward your goals. Help others along the way; allow yourself to be helped; and most importantly, serve.

This book is by no means a complete text on the principles of success. However, I hope it will entice you to read further. At the back of this book, I have attached a reading list of books that can further help you with your growth and development. I hope this book inspires you to continue reading, learning, and growing. Remember the acronym P.I.N.K. and share the principles with others. It's as simple as PASSION, INTEGRITY, NO LIMITS, and KNOWLEDGE. With P.I.N.K., the world can be yours!

> "My philosophy is that not only are you responsible for your life, but doing the best at this moment puts you in the best place for the next moment."
> — Oprah Winfrey

Recommended Reading

1. Secrets of Six-Figure Women – Barbara Stanny
2. Millionaire Women Next Door – Thomas Stanley, PH.D
3. The Girl's Guide to Being A Boss – Caitlin Friedman and Kimberly Yorio
4. Excuse Me, Your Life Is Waiting – Lynn Grabhorn
5. The Law of Attraction – Michael J. Losier
6. No Matter What – Lisa Nichols
7. How To Win Friends & Influence People – Dale Carnegie
8. What is Holding You Back – Sam Horn
9. Screw It, Let's Do It – Richard Branson
10. How To Choose Happiness ... Most of the Time – Chappale Linn Burton
11. The Magic of Thinking Big – David Schwartz
12. What Got You Here, Won't Get You There – Marshall Goldsmith
13. The Anatomy of Peace – Arbinger Institute
14. The Power of Now – Eckhart Tolle
15. Quantum Success – Sandra Anne Taylor

About the Author

Erica Moore-Burton, Esq.

Erica Moore-Burton, Esq., hails from London, England. She is an executive recruiter, professional speaker, and career coach. She arrived in the United States a little more than ten years ago with approximately $800 in her pocket. She used what she now calls the P.I.N.K. principles to navigate her way to personal and professional career success. She experienced several of her dream jobs before finding her calling of helping others to navigate their careers and personal lives. She climbed the corporate ladder quickly and went from an account executive to an executive director for a national employment search firm. Ms. Moore-Burton has worked with many prominent national law firms and corporate departments across the United States and is the recipient of several awards for her leadership and sales achievements (which were awarded to the top 3 percent of an organization with over 14,000 employees), as well as being recognized in the One-Million-Dollar club. She is the author of many published articles, including: How To Survive A Layoff and Get back on Track, Bend Don't Fold to Your Boss's Style, Ten Positive Developments on the Legal Scene, Build It And They Will Come, and The Reputation Ripple.